OCCULT
TIBET

YOUR WORLD DOES NOT EXIST!

Tibetan Buddhists believe your solid-seeming world is an illusion. Like the heroes of the movie *The Matrix,* a small number of them work hard to break through the illusion to the reality beyond, and some have high hopes that all of humanity will eventually realize the way things really are. They are also aware, from bitter personal experience, that simply believing the world to be unreal is not enough to change anything. Rigorous effort and yogic training are both required to break down the conditioning that holds us in our natural "matrix."

Most intriguing of all, Tibetan philosophers have tackled one of the most difficult questions to arise out of the doctrines of Buddhism: if all is illusion, what is the point of morality and correct behavior? Their answer is twofold. First, experience shows that correct behavior and morality are important in escaping the illusion. Secondly, those of us who remain locked in the unreal world of *sangsara* have no option but to obey its rules, just as those who failed to recognize the matrix for what it was were forced to function within its rigid program. While the illusion is maintained, we have the choice of generating positive karma and consequently improving the quality of our future life.

Tibetan sorcerers go one step further. Like the characters in *The Matrix,* they prefer the illusory world to the reality beyond, but study its mechanics in order to perform miracles. In essence, they believe that if our world is the product of mind, then control of the mind must lead to control of our environment; what is made by mind can be changed by mind.

— J. H. Brennan

ABOUT THE AUTHOR

J. H. (Herbie) Brennan is an acclaimed author of seventy books of fiction and nonfiction, several of which have become international bestsellers. His works have appeared in more than fifty countries of Europe, Asia, North and South America, and Australia. His *Grailquest* series of adventure gamebooks for young readers is a phenomenal success worldwide.

Brennan started his intellectual journey at an early age, studying psychology virtually from the time he could read, and hypnotizing a school friend at age nine! At twenty-four, he was the youngest newspaper editor in his native Ireland. By his mid-twenties, he had published his first novel, and his out-of-body experience work *Astral Doorways* is a classic in its field.

Herbie Brennan is clearly a man of ideas. In addition to his work an an author, he maintains an active interest in software development, self-improvement techniques, and reincarnation research. He is a frequent lecturer and media guest throughout the United Kingdom and Ireland.

TO WRITE TO THE AUTHOR

If you wish to contact the author or would like more information about this book, please write to the author in care of Llewellyn Worldwide and we will forward your request. Both the author and publisher appreciate hearing from you and learning of your enjoyment of this book and how it has helped you. Llewellyn Worldwide cannot guarantee that every letter written to the author can be answered, but all will be forwarded. Please write to:

J. H. Brennan
℅ Llewellyn Worldwide
P.O. Box 64383, Dept. 0-7387-0067-3
St. Paul, MN 55164-0383, U.S.A.

Please enclose a self-addressed stamped envelope for reply,
or $1.00 to cover costs. If outside U.S.A., enclose
international postal reply coupon.

Many of Llewellyn's authors have websites with additional information and resources. For more information, please visit our website at http://www.llewellyn.com.

J.H. BRENNAN

OCCULT TIBET

SECRET PRACTICES
OF HIMALAYAN MAGIC

2002
Llewellyn Publications
St. Paul, Minnesota 55164-0383, U.S.A.

First Edition
First Printing, 2002

Book design and editing by Joanna Willis
Cover background art © 2001 by Photodisc
Cover design by Kevin R. Brown

Library of Congress Cataloging-in-Publication Data
Brennan, J. H.
    Occult Tibet: secret practices of Himalayan magic / J.H. Brennan.—1st ed.
        p.   cm.
    Includes bibliographical references (p.) and index.
    ISBN 0-7387-0067-3
        1. Occultism—China—Tibet. I. Title.

    BF1434.C5 B74 2002
    133'.0951'5—dc21

                                                            2001050765

Llewellyn Publications
A Division of Llewellyn Worldwide, Ltd.
P.O. Box 64383, Dept. 0-7387-0067-3
St. Paul, MN 55164-0383, U.S.A.
www.llewellyn.com

Printed in the United States of America

ALSO BY J. H. BRENNAN

The Magical I Ching

Magick for Beginners

Time Travel

Magical Use of Thought Forms
(with Dolores Ashcroft-Nowicki)

To Jacks

CONTENTS

Contents

PREFACE

A *phurba* (sometimes transliterated *phurpa*) is an artifact of the Tibetan esoteric tradition. Strictly speaking it's a ritual dart, but it can sometimes take the form of a small knife. It is a purely magical weapon used for "killing" (in effigy) human or demonic foes. While various ceremonial items used in Tibetan Buddhism are now fairly easily available in the West, a genuine phurba remains a rarity. The first time I ever saw one was in 1998 and it led me into an interesting psychical adventure.

I was in Britain at the time travelling through the Cotswolds. My wife, who is almost as interested in Tibet as I am, recalled that some years ago she had read of a specialist company selling Tibetan goods in the area. We went searching and found a trea-sure trove.

The store was on two levels, one of which was almost entirely taken up by Tibetan carpets and rugs. The other displayed a mar-velous collection of artifacts. There were familiar items like prayer wheels, the wooden hand-held wheels with which Tibetans mech-anize prayer. The mantra *"Om mani padme hum"* is carved on the outside and also placed inside written on a tiny roll of paper. As the wheel spins, the mantra of compassion and peace is sent out to the universe.

I saw a selection of bells and *dorjes,* both of which have made their way to the West in large numbers. The dorje is a curious metal implement that comes in various sizes and looks vaguely like a miniature dumbbell (see illustration on page 66). A symbol of the Hindu god Indra, *dorje* translates as "thunderbolt." It is held in the right hand during ritual, invariably partnered by a bell which is held in the left. Together they mediate masculine and feminine energies.

Dorjes, bells, and prayer wheels are to be had in virtually any Asian souvenir shop, but in this outlet I soon began to note far more unusual items. Hanging from a low beam were several *damarus,* the small double drums used in Tibetan tantra in association with a trident known as a *trisula.* In its most esoteric form the damaru is crafted from two half-skulls, but these drums, to my relief, were of leather bound with thongs. Small pieces of wood and bone were attached to the ends of the thongs so that when the drum was twisted, they rattled against the drumheads with a distinctive sound. There was also a large selection of the singing bowls for which Tibet has become famous.

I was drawn to a wall display of several magnificent *thangkas.* These are protection paintings of the Buddha on silk with embroidered silk borders. They often incorporate the mandala motif that Carl Jung maintained was a symbol of psychic wholeness. Underneath the thangkas in a glass-fronted cabinet I noticed a *sankha,* an elaborately hand-carved conch shell that can be sounded to give a deep, throaty note. Once used as war trumpets, these shells found their way into Tibetan ritual as a proclamation of the glory of the saints and as a symbol of the gods because of the penetrating nature of their sound.

Beside the shell was another unusual item, a Tibetan *pustaka.* This is a hand-made copy of a sacred book printed on separate sheets with the aid of woodcut blocks and then bound between two boards with a single piece of ribbon.

I walked slowly through the rest of the store and examined *tingshaws* (cymbals), prayer lockets, prayer flags, *malas* (108-bead rosaries), and some beautiful *tashis* embroidered with the eight auspicious signs of Buddhism. In one cabinet I even noticed a *kangling*. This, more than anything else, emphasized that the establishment went well beyond tourist souvenirs. A kangling is a special trumpet used in tantric ceremonies to drive away evil spirits. It is made from a human thighbone.

Eventually I came upon an antique phurba hanging from a display peg. If the item had not been clearly labelled, I would never have recognized it. I had seen photographs of modern phurbas and they were exactly what you might expect: metal artifacts with short ornamental shafts and broad triangular blades. This thing looked nothing like them. It was made from bone and the blade was far slimmer than usual, it was rounded at the end, and held nothing of the familiar triangular shape. It was about the size of a pocketknife and the short, carved handle was finished off with a trailing black braid of what turned out to be human hair. The card underneath identified it as a monastic phurba originating in Tibet sometime prior to the Chinese invasion of October 1950. But apart from explaining how a phurba was typically used, the card gave no further information.

Although not exactly a collector of Tibetan memorabilia, I did have one or two ritual implements at home and was attracted by the idea of owning a genuine phurba. I took it down from its peg to examine it more closely.

I disliked the thing at once. The braid of human hair combined with a knobbed carving at the end of the handle gave it the appearance of a tiny doll—and a malevolent little doll at that. It was well within my means, but I decided there and then I would not buy it. I hung the phurba back on its peg and moved on to more attractive items.

That evening while dressing for dinner in our hotel room, I suddenly realized I was not looking forward to the meal. In fact, I was not looking forward to anything very much. I felt listless and curiously empty. This was odd. Although we were primarily in Britain for a meeting with a London publisher, the business part of the trip had been successfully completed days before. I was now on a holiday break. I normally enjoy sightseeing in England and the delights of good British restaurants. Yet with all this ahead of me, I felt flat, drained even, and if I was honest with myself, depressed.

I began to mentally backtrack over the day to find out when the trouble started. I soon realized the trigger had been touching the phurba.

This was an intriguing discovery. In a Hollywood movie, the plot would become instantly clear: the lama's curse, the malevolent artifact, the unwary victim . . . We all know those romantic stories of the explorer who steals the emerald eye from the pagan idol and meets with hauntings, misfortune, and death. Real life is seldom like that but I did begin to wonder if the original owner of the phurba had set an occult guardian on it perhaps to protect against theft. I had no way of knowing, but I did know how to deal with something of this sort. Suffice it to say I took the necessary steps and the depression lifted at once.

Trivial as this incident was, it served to remind me of the great esoteric tradition that developed in the Himalayan fastnesses of the Tibetan plateau. Over centuries of isolation, this unique culture investigated the mysteries of mind and magic to a degree never before attempted. Only the civilization of ancient Egypt came close to the understanding and insight developed in Tibet. Tibet was the magical capital of our planet.

Tibet underwent a profound change with the Chinese invasion of 1950. Until then, an astonishing 25 percent of the population was fully occupied with spiritual pursuits. But the monasteries dispatched no missionaries and for centuries the number of foreign visitors who reached Tibet was miniscule. (Just before the Second World War, there were only six Europeans in the entire country.) Tibet kept its secrets to itself.

When the People's Liberation Army marched across the border, the situation changed. Communist China agreed with Karl

Marx that religion is the opiate of the people. The new masters of Tibet saw the monasteries not as repositories of spiritual wisdom but as parasites supported by the sweat of ignorance and set about closing them down.[1] Many of those who had previously devoted their lives to an investigation of spiritual realities became forced labor for the new regime. China replaced the old religion with its own philosophy of materialism and did everything it could to break the back of traditional Tibetan culture.

This development, ugly and brutal though it was, had one positive aspect. While a long dark night settled over Tibet itself, the seeds of Tibetan spirituality began, for the first time in centuries, to be broadcast more widely. Centers of Tibetan culture were established by monastic refugees in America, Britain, Europe, and Ireland. Tibetan masters began to write their own books and explain the spiritual work and insights of their native country. Their teaching has been widely welcomed.

But if Tibetan spirituality is spreading, the same cannot be said for Tibetan magic. This body of techniques, based partly on Buddhist practice and partly on shamanic Bön (the aboriginal religion of Tibet), has scarcely been investigated by Western occultists. This is a pity because Tibetan magic, which in many of its aspects links seamlessly with Tibetan mysticism, has a great deal to teach the esoteric community of the West. Hopefully this book may give some small insight into just how much.

---

1. In later years a few were reopened . . . as tourist attractions.

INTRODUCTION:

TIBETAN LANGUAGE AND PRONUNCIATION

In 1956, the Chinese authorities set up a twelve-man committee to tackle the "problem" of the Tibetan language. The invaders had found themselves trying to cope with a tongue that had no word for important things like trucks, airplanes, electric generators, or atom bombs, yet was packed with different terms for incomprehensibly subtle levels of meditation and trance.

To compound their difficulties, the Chinese discovered a bewildering lack of generics. The Tibetans could, for example, speak of a poplar, spruce, or willow, yet lacked any word for the all-embracing term "tree."

The situation was further complicated by a multiplicity of language structures. To Chinese ears, the tongue of the monasteries sounded very different to the parlance of the common people. There was a language spoken only at court, full of honorifics denoting rank and respect. Wide gaps seemed to have sprung up between written Tibetan, which was clearly a religious language, and spoken Tibetan, which often concentrated on more mundane concerns. To make matters worse, there were regional differences

in pronunciation. Given that the written form reflected the pronunciation current when it was first introduced in the seventh
century, the dialects of western Tibet and Kham (to the east)
seemed closest to the source, while central Tibet and the capital
Lhasa showed a whole range of modifications.

Clearly something had to be done. The Chinese set themselves
on the task of establishing "standard Tibetan" based on the language of Lhasa. More than twenty years later, they admitted that
progress had proven "slow," although the invaders were optimistic
that their approved forms would "eventually" spread throughout
the population.

If the Chinese face problems, so, too, do Western scholars.
Tibetan and English do not share a common alphabet, so all English renderings of Tibetan terms are necessarily approximate.
Because of this—and, indeed, the pronunciation differences across
Tibet itself—there can be considerable variations in transliteration. For example, renderings like *Lying* and *Ling* both point
toward the same Tibetan original.

I have tried to keep transliterations in this book as simple as
possible, but even so there are likely to be pitfalls. The following
(very) rough guide to the pronunciation of Tibetan terms may
help readers avoid the worst of them.

The form *th* is not normally pronounced as a single sound as it is
in such common English words as "three," "though," "throw,"
and so on. Instead it is broken into its component sounds of *t* and
h as in "hot-house.' The same holds true for the usages *ph, dh,
kh,* and *jh.*

The letter *c* generally sounds like *ch* as in "child." The form *ch*
follows the usage outlined in the previous paragraph and is split
into its components so that it sounds like *ch-h,* as in "match-
head." The letter *j* is equivalent to the English *j* as in "joke."

Some common and highly specific Tibetan transliterations are
ts, which is pronounced as in "sigh**ts**"; *tsh,* which splits into the *ts*

sound followed by *h* as in "hall"; and *z* is usually pronounced as in "zero" but can sound like the *j* in French—for example, "bonjour." (Some transliteration systems accent the letter to differentiate between the two.)

Where Tibetan transliterations begin with groups of two or three consonants—like *gsang* ("secret") or *khor-lo* ("wheel")—the letters *b, d, g, h, l, m,* and *s* are silent. Of these, *d, l,* and *s* are also silent when they appear as a final consonant, although they tend to modify preceding vowels except for *i* and *e*.

Finally, adding *y* to *b, m, p,* or *ph* modifies their pronunciation. The usage *by* is equivalent to *j*; *my* becomes *ny* as in "canyon"; *py* is sounded *ch* as in "church"; while *phy* splits into *ch* and *h,* sounded as in "church-hall."

THE LAND THAT
TIME FORGOT

According to the most ancient of Tibetan scriptures, the human race did not evolve on Earth. We came from a distant galaxy to colonize this planet, but lost our memories and spacefaring abilities in the process.

In a creation tale unlike any other, the *Jigten Chagtsul* tells how an alien race evolved in a world at the center of the universe. This race was known as the *Lha* and their planet was beautiful, with hills, valleys, rivers, streams, trees, and flowers much like our own. On it, the Lha developed astounding powers but remained subject to old age and death. They lived mortal lives and disputed among themselves over possessions and property, much as humans do today.

The *Jigten Chagtsul* forms part of the *Chöjung*, a body of historical doctrine that was written down in the thirteenth century but which reflects a much older tradition. This doctrine describes not just the beginnings of our world, but of "all worlds." In passages oddly reminiscent of modern scientific findings, it speaks of

1

a void before time out of which a foam emerged to form the foundation of matter.[1]

The planet at the center of the universe was named the *Rirab Lhunpo*, after a massive mountain on its surface. Our own planet Earth was known as the *Dzambu Lying*, and began as an empty globe devoid of people, animals, or vegetation. Later it was colonized by members of the Lha who made it their own.

The extraordinary powers of the Lha ensured they lived in comfort. They practiced a form of deep meditation called *samten se* which enabled them to create matter, including food and useful artifacts, solely by the power of their minds. Their bodies glowed with an inner radiance.

Unfortunately, something in Earth's environment—the scriptures suggest it was an indigenous foodstuff to which the visitors took a liking—caused a weakening and eventual disappearance of the Lha's powers. They lost their inner radiance, along with the ability to create matter, and became the progenitors of the human race. The Lha, say these ancient Tibetan records, are our most distant ancestors.

Curiously, this mythic history is reflected in the traditions of the Dzopa, a tribe from the remote mountains of Baian-Kara-Ula on the Tibet-China border. These tiny people, who share none of the racial characteristics of their neighbors, claim they came from Sirius, a binary star in the constellation Canis Major some 8.6 light-years from Earth.

News of the Dzopa first emerged in 1938 when Chinese archaeologists discovered little human bones with disproportionately large skulls in a cave system of the Baian-Kara-Ula mountains. The bones were accompanied by artifacts in the form of stone discs with spiral grooves cut into their surfaces. These discs were

---

1. Big Bang theory postulates a primeval "atom" before which there was a timeless void. Quantum physics has discovered the most fundamental state of matter is a "quantum foam" of seething particles.

subsequently investigated by an Englishman, Dr. Karyl Robin-Evans, who travelled to China in 1947 after being shown one which he claimed lost and gained weight over a 3.5-hour cycle.

From China, Robin-Evans travelled to the Tibetan capital Lhasa, then on to the Baian-Kara-Ula mountains where he made contact with the Dzopa and learned their tribal history from a religious leader named Lurgan-La. According to this history, two expeditions had been sent to Earth from the Sirius star system. The first arrived more than twenty thousand years ago, and the second, much more recently, in 1014 C.E. Lurgan-La claimed his tribe originated with the second visit, which ended in disaster when the spaceship crashed.

In 1962, Dr. Tsum Um Nui of the Peking Academy of Prehistory claimed to have decoded the spiral engravings on the stone discs. He maintained they contained records of a spaceship that crashed to Earth twelve thousand years ago,[2] but the academic establishment failed to take his paper seriously.[3]

A more orthodox account of Tibetan prehistory suggests that some twenty million years ago the area that is now Tibet lay at the bottom of the sea.[4] Plate tectonics—the gradual movement of the Earth's surface—caused a slow, massive folding of the seabed into a series of parallel mountains. Alluvial silt eventually filled the valleys between the folds when rain-bearing winds from the Indian Ocean wore down the peaks. The result was the Tibetan plateau which rises to an average height of sixteen thousand feet above sea level.

The great Himalayan range that protects Tibet today was a more recent addition. The mountains certainly rose to their present

2. The contradiction in the dates suggests a lot more investigation needs to be done on the Dzopa, their traditions, and their mysterious stone discs.

3. Robin-Evans, *Sungods in Exile*.

4. By another of those weird coincidences that seem to dog the story of this strange land, Tibetan myth maintains that before the advent of humanity, the Tibetan plateau lay beneath a vast body of water and only saw the light of day when a bodhisattva drained it.

height within the last half-million years, and current geological investigation suggests they may be far more recent—the result of a massive cataclysmic upheaval dated no more than ten to twelve thousand years ago.

But whenever they rose, the Himalayas created Tibet as it is known today. The mountains form a twenty-four-thousand-foot-high barrier stretching 1,500 miles from east to west. It is a barrier that blocks the monsoon winds and has turned much of Tibet—and indeed central Asia as a whole—into a chill desert. It also put a stop to humanity's ancient migrations across the central Asian steppes and led to an isolation that has been Tibet's most dominant cultural characteristic for centuries. Until the Chinese invasion of October 1950, you could generally count the number of foreign residents in Tibet on the fingers of one hand.

A land will always sculpt its people. Isolation has been Tibet's predominant cultural characteristic; its most obvious physical characteristics are thin air and biting cold, and both have profound implications for those who live there. When the London *Times* correspondent Perceval Landon visited Phag Ri, Tibet's highest settlement, in 1904, he found a ramshackle village of listless, unwashed inhabitants. An open sewer in the center of the main street contained excrement, offal, and the corpses of long-dead dogs in a hideous mixture that scarcely maintained its slow, curdled flow.

The characteristic listlessness sprang from oxygen deprivation. At eighteen thousand feet, Phag Ri was not only the highest town in the country, but in the world. Even Tibetans found it difficult to cope with the thin air. The appalling state of public and personal hygiene was compounded by the listlessness, but sprang mainly from the lack of free water, most of which was locked up as ice all year round. The open sewer flowed only due to the latent heat of the excrement it contained. In the barren land, fuel was at a premium. What little there was had to be preserved for essentials like cooking. Water for washing was a luxury. Bathing was unthinkable.

Phag Ri is an extreme example, but remained typical of pre-invasion Tibet in its hygiene standards. Yet despite such conditions, there was comparatively little infectious illness in the country and the great plagues that killed millions in neighboring India and China were unheard of in Tibet. This was partly due to the low population density, but a far more important factor was the cold—bacteria simply do not thrive.

Once attention is focused on the cold, the thin air, the rocky, inhospitable, infertile land, and the lack of natural resources such as oil, coal, or timber, certain developments become predictable. The first is a small population. The land will not support the teeming millions of India or China. The second is long-term cultural stability, possibly declining into stagnation. Once a balance is reached between population and resources, there is little incentive to change old ways of doing things, and no money to spare for major changes anyway.

An examination of Tibetan history shows these factors clearly. Although impoverished by Western standards, Tibet never faced famine. Largely unaware of the world outside, its people saw nothing of which to be envious. There was no incentive to change and the country remained a feudal monarchy, albeit of an unusual type, until change was forced upon it by external intervention.

But contrary to its modern image, Tibet was not always a peace-loving country. For centuries there was a constant ebb and flow of military campaigns with neighboring China. Tibetan warlords gained the upper hand as often as their Chinese counterparts, but in the twentieth century, China modernized its military machine while Tibet did not. By this time, Tibet had long since initiated an experiment unique in the modern world. As a culture, it had embarked on a spiritual path that precluded the use of violence.

Most scholars attribute the first hesitant steps on this path to the arrival of Buddhism in the seventh century C.E. Tibetan chronicles record the event in a suitably miraculous context. According to these sources, an early century king named Lhato Thori was on the roof of his palace in Tibet when an enormous casket fell from the sky at his feet. Inside were certain religious scriptures, a scale model of a golden tomb, and the six sacred syllables of what became the Tibetan Prayer of Everlasting Truth.

Although the Bönpoba (practitioners of Tibet's aboriginal Bön religion) claim the miraculous scriptures as their own, they are more widely believed to have been the Buddhist *Dunkong Shakgyapa*. Buddhist or Bön, the illiterate king was unable to read them, but he was able to recognize a good omen when it fell from the sky. Thus he stored the chest away safely and embarked on a daily worship of the books, a practice that doubled his life span to 120 years.

(The idea that Tibetan mystics discovered the secret of longevity has proved remarkably persistent. In James Hilton's popular romance *The Lost Horizon,* residents of Shangri-La, a Himalayan kingdom based on Tibet, remained youthful for centuries so long as they did not venture from their valley home.)

Shortly after he began his religious discipline, King Lhato Thori was visited by the Buddha in a dream. The Buddha told him that the secret of the books would remain hidden to him, but after five generations a stranger would explain the texts to the people. Here, too, we find an ancient reflection of Tibetan esoteric practice which, as we shall also see later, makes very interesting use of dreams.

Five generations later, the prophecy came true. In the second decade of the seventh century, King Srontsan Gampo decided the strange scriptures inherited from his predecessor should be translated into Tibetan and dispatched a team of seventeen scholars to India in search of instruction. At the time Tibet had no written language but one of the scholars, a government minister named

Thonmi Sambhoto, actually devised one, a monumental achievement loosely based on the Kashmiri *Sharada* alphabet.

Once this hurdle was crossed, not only was the secret of the ancient *Dunkong Shakgyapa* revealed, but a great many other scriptures, both Buddhist and Hindu, were translated into Tibetan. Although King Srontsan Gampo was a Bön practitioner, he was strongly attracted to the new religion. When he subsequently married two Buddhist princesses—one from Nepal, the other from China—he decided to convert. In this way, Buddhism was introduced into Tibet, and while for a time it remained confined to the royal family, it eventually spread.

For anyone brought up within the revealed religions of Christianity, Judaism, or Islam, Buddhism is a strange doctrine. It denies not only the existence of God, but of a human soul. It teaches reincarnation—the great wheel of birth, death, and rebirth—but believes an individual's greatest aspiration is to cease to incarnate. Above all, its practitioners follow the Buddha's central precept, "Seek your own salvation with diligence."

This precept has given the religion enormous flexibility and led it to adapt to the prevailing conditions of different countries as it spread. Sometimes the adaptation has been extreme. Buddhism as practiced in Japan (under the name of Zen) bears little resemblance to its Indian root. Buddhism as practiced in Tibet was to share the same fate.

In an attempt to explain the emergence of Bön in his country, the Dalai Lama's older brother Abbot Thubten Jigme Norbu had this to say:

> Every traveller who has set foot in Tibet has commented on the wild countryside. . . . It is a country that can be so still and quiet and so beautiful that even we who have been born in it . . . are affected strongly. [But] just as it can be quiet, it can also be so tumultuous that it seems as though the world were coming to an end. . . . If the country is powerful in its quiet moments, it is

something much more than powerful when it is black. . . . Living in a world like this, it is difficult not be become dominated by it.⁵

There seems little doubt that Bön emerged in reaction to the country of its birth exactly as the abbot suggests, but so, too, did Buddhism. Indeed there are so many similarities between Buddhism and Bön it is often difficult to tell them apart. Thubten Jigme Norbu again:

> There is no way of telling whether a man is a Bönpoba or a Buddhist when you meet him. His clothes, his manner of speech, his behaviour, all are the same as our own. Inside his house the altar might be a little different . . .⁶

Like Buddhism, the Bön religion had its monasteries. Both types of monasteries were organized in exactly the same way. Monks in each took exactly the same number of vows—253. It is clear that Bön borrowed from Buddhism. It is equally clear that in Tibet, Buddhism borrowed from Bön. Tibetan occultism drew heavily on both traditions and permeated the entire culture. Until the Chinese invasion, the government was a reincarnatory monarchy whose decisions were guided by spirit voices speaking through a state oracle. A communications system had been developed using entranced runners and, according to some sources at least, telepathy. Prior to 1950, Tibet was arguably the strangest place on Earth. How did all this strangeness come about?

Abbot Norbu struck the right chord when he was speaking about Bön. Tibet is a wilderness of extremes. The beauty of the country is breathtaking. The stillness is profound, the silence almost tangible. It positively calls the human soul to meditate. But Tibet is also wild. It is subject to earthquakes that are capa-

---

5. Norbu and Turnbull, *Tibet*.
6. Ibid.

ble of swallowing whole villages. Although the monsoons are blocked by the mountains, there are storms of such violence that a hillside—and anyone on it—can be washed away in a matter of minutes. When the wind howls, the noise seems to fill the universe. As the abbot says, it is only human nature that the people who live in such a country will do their best to develop shamanic systems designed to control its natural forces.

But there is another, even more interesting, factor that comes into play. There is a phenomenon well known in the world of high-altitude mountaineering. Those who engage in the sport call it the "unseen companion." Climber after climber, including several engaged in Everest expeditions, has reported the eerie sensation of being accompanied by something or someone on the final stages of their climb, even though no one was actually there. Rather more controversially, one or two have even claimed that the unseen presence seemed to help them when they got into trouble, and protected them against the worst effects of blizzards by guiding their footsteps back to safety.

The occultist Aleister Crowley, no mean mountaineer himself, learned the unseen companion had a negative side when he tackled Himalayan peak K2, known locally as Kanchenjunga, the second highest mountain in the world. Although Crowley was courageous to the point of stupidity when climbing, he met with something on Kanchenjunga that terrified him. At least one of his biographers, the British author John Symonds, has assumed Crowley was personifying the mountain—a particularly treacherous peak that has killed a number of climbers—when he referred to the "Kanchenjunga Demon," but it is far more likely that he was speaking about an experience of the unseen companion.

The phenomenon manifests when mountaineers venture into high altitudes without oxygen equipment or when their equipment fails. This has led to the assumption that the experience is essentially a hallucination brought on by oxygen deprivation—a variation on the altitude sickness experienced by some tourists visiting destinations like Nepal. The locals take a different view. To them, the unseen companion is exactly what it seems to be: a disembodied entity that attaches itself, for good or ill, to those who enter its domain.

It is tempting to dismiss the local view as superstition, but is perhaps a little rash. Aldous Huxley, the British intellectual, experimented with mescaline (also known as peyote) and subsequently wrote a fascinating account of the experience in which he discussed the theory of "mind-at-large." According to this theory, the human mind is not generated by the physical brain as so many Western scientists assume. Rather it is something above and beyond the body which is aware of reality at a far deeper level than most of us experience. The brain acts as a "reducing valve," filtering out those impressions which are not useful for the job of survival. Mystical consciousness is all very well, but you might easily walk under a bus while contemplating the beauties of an expanded universe.

Huxley theorized that psychedelic substances like mescaline and many spiritual pursuits including yoga breathing all reduce the efficiency of the brain as a filter mechanism, allowing more impressions of mind-at-large to flood in. Far from these impressions being hallucinatory, they are intimations of reality levels we cannot normally access.

During the latter part of the 1960s, a series of experiments carried out by the distinguished British neurophysiologist Dr. W. Grey Walter lent indirect support to the theory of mind-at-large. Although his findings have been largely ignored, his work showed conclusively that mind, whatever it may be, cannot be a product of the brain.

Grey Walter's experimental procedure was based on the fact that the human brain generates measurable electrical signals. He attached electrodes to the scalps of volunteers over the area of the frontal cortex. These electrodes amplified electrical activity and sent the signals on to a specially constructed machine. There was a button before the subject which caused an interesting scene to appear on a TV screen whenever it was pressed.

When you decide to take any physical action—including the pressing of a button—there is a twenty-microvolt electrical surge across your frontal cortex. Specialists call this a "readiness wave." Grey Walter amplified this readiness wave so that it could trigger the TV picture a fraction of a second before the button was actually pressed.

Subjects usually figured out what was happening fairly quickly and trained themselves to "will" the pictures onto the screen without touching the button. For this trick to work, the subject had to duplicate his or her mindset in pressing the button. Once the knack was developed, subjects could will pictures onto the screen directly, then dismiss them with the relevant thought when finished.

The appearance of screen pictures was not mind acting directly on matter since the switch was triggered by the amplified electrical surge originating in the subject's brain. But once subjects learned how to produce the pictures without pressing the button, their minds *were* directly influencing matter—the physical matter of their own brains. A decision of the mind, applied in a particular way, was all it took to change the electrical potential of the frontal cortex.

Grey Walter's experiments showed conclusively that it is the mind that controls the brain and not the other way around.[7] The implications are far-reaching. Among them is the realization that mind-at-large can no longer be dismissed as a mystical fantasy.

In the Tibetan context, this may mean that the country's basic geographical features—notably its thin air—created over the

---

7. The conclusion was confirmed in 2000 when scientific research in Scotland showed that in rare cases where flatline (brain-dead) patients were revived, many reported memories, which indicated that their minds had somehow survived the (temporary) demise of their brains.

generations a people who were constitutionally attuned to levels of reality normally hidden from the rest of us. It was this that led to the national obsession with religion and the development of occult technologies more profound and far-reaching than those of any other country. It was this that made Tibet a land of miracles and mysteries. Many of those miracles and mysteries were very strange indeed.

2

MYSTERIES
OF TIBET

Sometime during the fifteenth century, a curious document began
to circulate in Buddhist countries. It was the biography of a
Tibetan born near the border with Nepal in 1052. He was the son
of a merchant who happened to be away from home at the time
of the birth. When the merchant heard the news, he named his 2
son Thopaga, which means "delightful to hear." Although this
was probably meant to reflect the father's pleasure at the good
tidings, the boy himself proved delightful to hear. He developed a
fine singing voice and liked to use it spontaneously, breaking into
song on many occasions. 3

But after this auspicious beginning, Thopaga's life story took a
decidedly dark turn. At age seven, Thopaga lost his father. It was
a devastating blow and worse was to come. A greedy uncle 4
promptly confiscated the family inheritance and turned Thopaga,
his mother, and sister out of their home to fend for themselves.

Tibet is a hard country and Thopaga's mother found it hard to
survive with two small children. She managed somehow, but not

14

without building up a store of great bitterness and resentment toward her brother-in-law. The bitterness was shared by Thopaga who eventually took to alcohol as a way of deadening his emotional pain. At age seventeen he came home drunk one day to his disapproving mother and when she chastized him for his state, he promised he would do anything she asked to make amends. Suddenly all her pent-up resentment boiled over and she ordered him to find a sorcerer who would teach him the black magic needed for retribution on his uncle.

In the eleventh century as in the twentieth, Tibetan belief in black magic was widespread and there were many individuals who claimed dark powers. One of them was a lama named Yungtun-Trogyal[1] who had a fearsome reputation and was credited with the ability to raise storms and cause death at a distance. Thopaga asked to become his pupil and the lama agreed. After a lengthy period of apprenticeship, Thopaga was ready to take his revenge.

Thopaga waited until the wedding day of one of his cousins, a child of the uncle who had so wronged his mother and him. Weddings in Tibet are cause for great celebration, and guests travel many miles to attend. When everyone was assembled, Thopaga used techniques taught him by Yungtun-Trogyal to fill the house with vermin, then caused it to collapse. Thirty-five people died, but the biography[2] claimed that Thopaga spared his uncle and aunt "so that they might endure more suffering." Urged on by his mother who was far from satisfied by the nightmare wedding, Thopaga conjured a hailstorm to destroy his uncle's crops and thus effectively ruin him.

Although Thopaga claimed to regret his actions afterward, he remained in Yungtun-Trogyal's service for many years and was

---

1. This was evidently not the name he was born with—it translates as "wrathful and victorious teacher of evil."
2. Perhaps the best source in English is W. Y. Evans-Wentz's excellent *Tibet's Great Yogi Milarepa: A Biography from the Tibetan.*

approaching middle age before he finally decided to abandon the black arts. In a complete reversal of his former values, he apprenticed himself to a teacher named Marpa, the founder of the Kargyut-pa School of Tibetan Buddhism and a man widely regarded as a saint. Marpa refused to initiate his new pupil until he had atoned for his past sins and for a six-year period subjected Thopaga to a rigorous regime of regular beatings and back-breaking tasks. One of these tasks involved repeatedly building and tearing down a stone house.[3] It was not until Thopaga was forty-four that Marpa decided he had atoned for his sins and granted him the initiation he sought.

Thopaga then became as great a force for good as he had previously been for evil. On the death of his mother, which he foresaw in a dream, he vowed to devote his life to the ultimate spiritual goal. For a Buddhist like Thopaga, existence was governed by the Law of Karma. Crudely stated, it insists that present thoughts and actions absolutely determine your future state. Like virtually all Tibetans, he also believed implicitly in reincarnation. Against this background, the ultimate spiritual goal is liberation from the cycle of birth, death, and rebirth generated by karmic action. The liberated state, which involves experience of the mystical reality behind appearances, is called nirvana, although Tibetans often use the phrase "entering the clear light."

Although nirvana is seen as a perfectly legitimate reward for spiritual labor, Thopaga not just vowed he would attempt to achieve it, but that if he did, he would renounce his personal liberation until all other sentient beings had achieved enlightenment as well. In other words, he was determined to become a Buddha.[4]

---

3. This structure, in southern Tibet, was still standing in the twentieth century.

4. Most Westerners assume there is only one Buddha, but this is not so. Prince Gautama, who founded the religion known as Buddhism some five hundred years before the birth of Christ, was only one in a chain of Buddhas past and present. The term means "Enlightened One."

In pursuit of his goal, Thopaga took up residence in the White Cave of the Horse's Tooth, a high mountain cavern where he was unlikely to be disturbed in his meditations. To survive the bitter cold, he became adept in the practice of *tumo*, a mental discipline that generates great body heat. Henceforth he wore only a light cotton robe, known in Tibetan as a *repa*, which was to give him the name by which he is best known today—Milarepa.

In the high cavern, Milarepa's sole food was a soup made from nettles which eventually gave his skin and hair a greenish tinge. Over the years he developed curious powers. He was able to leave his body at will and travel anywhere he wished, not only in this world, but in other levels of reality. He became a shapeshifter with the ability to metamorphose into various animals, birds, or even such things as a flame or a stream. There were claims that he could levitate.

As word of his abilities began to spread, Milarepa found the remoteness of his cave no longer protected him from unwelcome visitors, so he moved to an area near Mount Everest. There a lama who was jealous of Milarepa's fame sent him a gift of poisoned curds. Milarepa's psychism alerted him, but he explained to the messenger that while poison could no longer affect him, he was, at eighty-four, ready to leave this world anyway. He gathered together his disciples and preached to them for several days about karma and the nature of reality. Then he sank into *samadhi*, a trance-like state recognized as the prelude to nirvana, and died.

According to the biography, there were postmortem miracles. Milarepa revived his own corpse, then resurrected in a second body which sang hymns amidst the flames of his funeral pyre before entering the clear light. Flowers rained down while comets streaked across the sky and formed themselves into a mandala. When the flames of the pyre died there was no sign of Milarepa's bones or ashes—they had been carried off by *dakini* spirits.

At first glance we might be tempted to see Milarepa's story as a medieval myth, one of those spiritualized legends full of magic and miracles that sometimes encrust an actual historical character. Something of this sort happened in the West when the romance of Camelot pervaded a "King" Arthur who may have been little more than a tribal chieftain. But while mandala skies and singing corpses are certainly unlikely, it may be rash to dismiss the whole story.

Milarepa's biography continues to be an inspiration to Buddhists to this day, but how much, if any, of it, could actually be true? Over the centuries since the story first began to circulate, there have been few Western visitors to bear witness to Tibet's marvels. And of the handful who did manage to visit the country, fewer still were interested. When, for example, the Younghusband Expedition marched on Lhasa in 1903, the accompanying London *Times* correspondent Perceval Landon noted they had passed the cave of a hermit who had resided in isolation for several years. Today there would be some appreciation of the man's spiritual fortitude. In 1903, Landon dismissed him as leading "a life wasted on empty superstition."[5]

But all this changed in 1916, due to the efforts of one remarkable woman. Louise Eugene Alexandra Marie David was born in Paris in 1868 but brought up in Brussels, Belgium, from the age of five. Unlike the *Times* correspondent, she developed an interest in the occult at an early age. She was just fifteen when she was first exposed to esoteric thought through the publications of a secret society in London that went under the name of the Supreme Gnosis. Five years later when she went to study in Britain, she stayed at Supreme Gnosis headquarters and learned something of Spiritualist, Rosicrucian, and Theosophical thought.

When Alexandra David was twenty-one, she returned to the European continent to study at the Sorbonne in Paris and boarded with a Theosophist family in the Latin Quarter. It was here that her interest in Buddhism awakened.

---

5. Landon, *Lhasa*.

Alexandra David made her first trip to the Far East when she was only twenty-three—she spent a small legacy travelling to India and Sri Lanka (then known as Ceylon). The journey gave her her first sight of the Himalayas that were to become so important to her later life. In 1904, she married an engineer named Philip Neel and while they parted company after just two years, they remained married and Philip supplied financial support for her well into her later life. It was Philip's money that allowed her to travel again and she returned to India in 1911. There she started an affair with the crown prince of Sikkim.

Sikkim, which is one of the smallest of the Indian states, is located in the eastern Himalayas and directly borders on Tibet. Alexandra David-Neel was immediately fascinated by Tibet and its customs. Through her lover, the crown prince, she met with lamas from both the major branches of Tibetan Buddhism (Red Hat and Yellow Hat sects), and in April 1912 had her first audience with the Dalai Lama.

The Dalai Lama was one of the strangest monarchs in the world not in himself, but in his office. He was both the spiritual and political head of Tibet, and was believed to be an aspect of Chenresig, the patron god of the country, and his own thirteenth incarnation. That description needs a little explanation.

Like the people of India, Tibetans accepted without question that reincarnation—rebirth after death in another body—was a fact of life. But this was no mere intellectual acceptance. Among the severely practical applications of the belief was the fact that you might contract a legally binding debt payable in your next life.

With such a mindset, it was hardly surprising that for generations Tibetans had declined to accept that death should interrupt the good governance of their country. Thus when any Dalai Lama died, they set out at once to find his reincarnation. The process was complex.

First, the dying Dalai Lama drew on a lifetime of spiritual training in an attempt to predict the direction in which his soul

might fly in its search for a new body.[6] Then, after death had
occurred, the state oracle was consulted. The British pilot
Robert Ford described the oracle as ". . . gesticulating, gyrating, ⟨4⟩
and beating his breast, hissing, groaning, and gnashing his
teeth, foaming at the mouth like an epileptic."[7] Despite this,
lamas in attendance on this spectacular trance medium usually
managed to make some sense of his messages which would contain further clues to where the dead Dalai Lama might have
reappeared.

Expeditions were then dispatched to search out suitable candidates, marked sometimes by omens, sometimes by signs such
as birthmarks or moles matching those of the old Dalai Lama.
These candidates, usually discovered as young children, would
then be tested. We know the sort of tests used since the present
fourteenth Dalai Lama in exile has described those that sealed
his own authenticity. A notable from the old Dalai Lama's court
came to examine him, but was disguised as a servant, while the
apparent leader of the party was a servant decked out in impres- ⟨5⟩
sive finery. The little boy recognized the real leader at once.
When offered a choice of items, he picked only those that had
belonged to the old Dalai Lama. When the investigators decided
they had discovered the genuine reincarnation—there were various candidates at the time—the boy was taken from his home
and brought to Lhasa for monastic training.

This—the thirteenth Dalai Lama—was the monarch who
granted Madame David-Neel audience. He told her firmly she
should learn Tibetan. Interestingly, around this time a *naljorpa*
(Tibetan magician) advised her to ignore the law that banned
foreigners from his country and seek initiation from a spiritual

---

6. Buddhism actually teaches *anata,* the doctrine that notions of a soul are illu-
sional, but many Buddhists are happy to function as if the soul existed.

7. Ford, *Captured in Tibet.*

master. Alexandra took the Dalai Lama's advice, but not the magician's. Instead, she returned to Sikkim.

The outbreak of the First World War in 1914 effectively imprisoned Alexandra in that country—there was no way she could return to Europe. But she had far more personal problems. The Crown Prince Sidkeong died unexpectedly and she was abruptly cut off from the luxurious life at court she had led as his lover. Instead of bemoaning her fate, she took the change of circumstances as a golden opportunity and apprenticed herself to the Great Hermit (Gomchen) of Lachen. This saintly individual lived in the Cave of the Clear Light some twelve thousand feet above sea level in the Himalayas. Alexandra pledged herself to absolute obedience and took up residence in a cave a mile away from his.

At this point, we have modern confirmation that some of Milarepa's ancient story might literally be true. Among the techniques taught to Alexandra by the Gomchen was the practice of tumo, the body-heat yoga used by Milarepa to survive the biting chill of the Tibetan highlands. Amazingly it worked and, as we shall see, enabled Alexandra to endure conditions just as extreme as any Milarepa ever faced.

In 1916, Alexandra entered Tibet for the first time. Although she did so at the invitation of the Panchen Lama, a monk second only in authority to the Dalai Lama, her trip enraged the authorities in British India and she was expelled from Sikkim on her return. She made her way to Japan, then China, and from there returned to Tibet.

Alexandra spent more than two years in the monastery of Kumbum, then in 1921 embarked on a perilous three-year journey to the Tibetan capital Lhasa. It was here her tumo training came into its own, for it enabled her to survive treks through deep snow, nights in freezing caves, and recurring bouts of illness. She arrived in Lhasa in February of 1924, but was disappointed with the city and left again in April. By 1925 she was back in France.

Chapter 2

Between 1925 and her death in 1969 (at the age of 100), Alexandra published numerous articles and several books about her experiences. Because of her profound interest in esoteric matters, this
body of work contains accounts of psychical and spiritual phenomena recorded in very few other sources. She speaks, for example, of
the telepathic link she achieved with the Gomchen of Lachen,
believed by Tibetans to be the finest way to receive high spiritual
teachings. She seems, too, to have undergone the mystic rite of
Chöd, an astonishing self-sacrifice to demonic forces which leads
ultimately to liberation from all attachments. And among other
remarkable sights she claimed to have seen one of Tibet's famous
lung-gom-pa runners and even a *tulpa*.

According to tradition, lung-gom-pa runners were able to
lighten their bodies and perhaps levitate in order to carry messages over vast distances across rough terrain. The runner
Alexandra David-Neel saw did not levitate, but bounded along
with a curious loping gait almost like a bouncing ball, and
appeared to be entranced.

The tradition of the tulpa was a lot more eerie. The belief was
that intense visualization and concentration on, for example, a
religious image could eventually make the mental picture visible
to others. Indeed, in certain circumstances the image could take
on a life of its own and behave in many respects like a ghost.
Madame David-Neel saw her first tulpa when a young painter
entered her camp. The man had a special devotion to a particular Tibetan deity, which he had painted many times and visualized even more often in the course of his meditations. Madame
David-Neel saw the etherial but perfectly visible figure of the
god looming behind the painter.

Madame David-Neel was not the only European visitor to bring
stories of strange phenomena back from Tibet in the twentieth
century. Theodor Illion, a German traveller with rather less sympa-
thy for the occult, nonetheless confirmed her reports about body-
heat tumo (although he failed to find the technique particularly

marvelous). He claimed, "The absolute reality of thought-transmission over fairly long distances and certain other less striking phenomena, such as psychometry and the like, is unquestionable."[8] He suspected the use of hypnosis by Tibetan sorcerers to make people "see" things that did not exist, and added the intriguing observation that some psychical phenomena was weather dependent—psychometry was adversely effected by rain, for example—while others that worked perfectly well at ten thousand feet would not work at all at thirteen thousand.

There have also been other, less easily verified reports about a mysterious Tibetan technology of sound which, while it did not survive in its totality into the twentieth century, nevertheless left some fascinating traces. The prime source of these reports is a work titled *Försvunnen teknik* by the Swedish author Henry Kjellson, published in 1961. At the time of this writing (2002), I have failed to locate an English language edition of the book, but the publisher Nihil in Copenhagen issued a Danish translation in 1974 and the British author Andrew Collins drew on this for his own account in *Gods of Eden* (Headline, 1998).

What Kjellson had to report was fascinating. He told of a Swedish doctor known simply as "Jarl" who was invited by a Tibetan friend during the 1930s to visit a monastery southwest of Lhasa. During his stay, Jarl was taken to a nearby cliff. About 250 meters up the cliff face was a cave entrance fronted by a broad ledge. Here the monks were engaged in building a stone wall.

As you might imagine, this was no easy site to reach. The only access to the cave was with ropes, which the monks had strung down from the top of the cliff. Jarl saw no sign of lifting machinery for the stones, but about the same distance from the base of the cliff as the ledge was above it there was a large, bowl-shaped boulder embedded in the ground. Behind it was a substantial

---

8. Illion, *In Secret Tibet.*

Chapter 2

group of monks. Jarl's attention was drawn to several of the monks who carried large drums and long trumpets.

As Jarl watched, a monk used a knotted piece of measuring rope to position thirteen drums and six trumpets in a ninety-degree arc around the bowl-stone. About ten monks formed a line behind each instrument while there were five more monks with drums at the center of the arc. The middle man had a small drum hung around his neck. The monks on either side of him had larger drums hung from wooden frames, while on either side of these were monks holding three-meter-long trumpets. Beyond them were even more drums slung from frames, one pair being the largest Jarl ever saw. Further out along the arc drums alternated with trumpets. All the drums were open at one end and this end was pointed toward the bowl-stone.

A sled drawn by a yak dragged a large stone block to the bowl-stone where it was manhandled into the depression by a group of monks. The monk at the center of the arc then began to chant and beat the small drum. The rhythm was taken up by the trumpets, then the larger drums, and gradually increased in pace until the sound seemed continuous.

This went on for three or four minutes. Then the block in the center of the bowl-stone wobbled. As it did so, the monks slowly tilted their instruments—both trumpets and drums—upward. The block rose with them as if levitated by the sound and followed an arced trajectory toward the cave-mouth high above. When it reached the ledge, the players stopped and the stone crashed down ready for use in the wall. Another block was then dragged to the bowl-stone.

Kjellson reported further evidence of Tibetan levitation by sound in the experience of an Austrian moviemaker he called "Linauer." Linauer also visited a remote Tibetan monastery in the 1930s. There he was shown an enormous gong made up of a golden center section ringed with hoops of iron and brass. He was also shown a bowl-shaped stringed instrument (rather like an open lute) two meters long and one meter wide, which, like the gong, was cast using three different metals. The thing was so large it had to be supported by a wooden frame.

The gong and the bowl were used together with two large screens set to form a triangle. When the gong was struck, it set up sympathetic vibrations in the strings of the bowl. The screens directed the sound toward a large stone block. After repeatedly striking the gong, a monk was able to lift the block with one hand, even though it appeared far too heavy. The monk claimed that "long ago" instruments of this type had been used to build defensive walls "round the whole of Tibet."[9] He also said that similar devices emitted sounds that would shatter stone and dissolve matter.

9. Collins, *Gods of Eden*.

Chapter 2

3

SONIC SECRETS

What are we to make of all this? Although Alexandra David-Neel was a respected witness—she received the French Legion of Honor, the Gold Medal of the French Geographical Society, the Silver Medal of the Royal Belgian Geographical Society, and the Insignia of the Chinese Order of the Brilliant Star—her stories of Tibet remain fantastic. Henry Kjellson reports on Tibetan phenomena second hand and does not even give the full names of his witnesses. Theodor Illion's assertions about telepathy and psychometry are backed by little hard evidence.

There is no doubt at all that Tibet is just the sort of remote, little-known land that generates romantic legends.[1] One, for example, tells how Jesus Christ quarrelled with his parents and ran away to India from whence, after several years, he entered Tibet and studied Buddhism at the Hemis Monastery in the town of Ladakh. Eventually he returned to his own country to

---

1. Peter Bishop makes this point persuasively in his *Dreams of Power* (Athlone Press, 1993), a book that traces the impact of Tibet on Western imagination.

preach a new religion. Is the story true? We have no way of knowing. The source manuscript was reputedly taken from the monastery by a Russian visitor and while he sent back a translation, this, too, was stolen by some foreign traveller.

All the same, it would be unwise to dismiss every Tibetan story as nonsense, however bizarre it might seem at first sight. An example is the comment that ended our last chapter. It seems ludicrous to suggest sound might have the capacity to dissolve matter and shatter stone. Yet the British biologist and author Dr. Lyall Watson reports in his book *Supernature* on an incident in France that demonstrates exactly this phenomenon in modern times.

According to Watson, an engineering professor named Gavraud was subject to recurring bouts of nausea while at work in his institute in Marseilles. The sickness became so bad that he was on the point of giving up his job. The only thing that stopped him was the suspicion that it was something in his environment that was causing the trouble. He began to run tests.

His first thought was chemical pollutants. At the time (early 1970s) there had been problems with the constituents of certain building materials and some fabric cleaners. But tests for the more likely culprits proved negative. Professor Gavraud then tested for more obscure chemicals and even radioactivity, still with negative results. He was on the point of giving up when chance intervened. Leaning against a wall of his office, which was on the top floor of the building, he became aware of a slight vibration. Soon he realized the whole room was filled with a very low frequency subsonic hum.

Gavraud set about tracing the hum to its source and discovered the root cause was an air conditioning plant on the roof of the building opposite. By sheer coincidence it happened that his office was exactly the right shape and distance away to resonate with the machinery. The basic rhythm—seven cycles a second—was what was making him ill.

Chapter 3

The discovery fascinated Gavraud. He decided to build something that could generate infrasound so he could investigate it further. He cast about for a likely prototype and found that the standard-issue police whistle carried by all gendarmes actually generated a whole range of low frequency sounds. Using this as a model, he built a police whistle six feet long powered by compressed air.

When the device was tested—by a technician rather than Gavraud himself—Tibetan theories about the destructive power of sound were dramatically vindicated. On the first blast, the technician collapsed. Medical examination showed he had died instantly. A postmortem reported his internal organs had been turned to jelly.

Despite the tragedy, Gavraud pressed on with his experiments, but with precautions. His next test was conducted outdoors and the observers were sheltered in a concrete bunker. The compressed air was turned on very gradually, but even so the sound broke every window within a half mile of the test site.

Before long, Gavraud learned how to control the amplitude of the sound vibrations and also how to build much smaller infrasound generators. He also discovered that the sound could be specifically focused. By directing two sound beams at a target building, the structure could be demolished at distances up to five miles. Gavraud registered patents on several of his devices and it seems likely that it will be only a matter of time before French military authorities begin to take an interest, if they have not already done so.

While the Gavraud experiments are strong confirmation of Tibetan claims about the destructive power of sound, it is less easy to take seriously the idea that sound can also be used to affect the weight of solid objects and even levitate massive stone blocks. All the same, there seems to be some confirmation of these claims as well.

John Ernst Worrell Keely was born in Chester, Pennsylvania, or possibly Philadelphia, in either 1827 or 1837. The difficulties in determining exactly where or when recur when dealing with the remainder of Keely's colorful biography. He is a man almost impossible to pin down, someone whose life was built on flamboyant claims, and not all of them easy to substantiate. The 1998 electronic edition of the *Encyclopedia Britannica* describes him simply—but perhaps not definitively—as "a fraudulent American inventor."

According to *Free Energy Pioneer* by Theo Paijmans, Keely was not overeducated. He left school at the age of twelve to become a carpenter's apprentice. But woodwork was never his real interest. He later claimed that even before the age of ten he was investigating "acoustic physics"—the power of sound. In 1872, he startled the world with an announcement of a new energy source.

Keely's new energy, "inter-molecular vibrations of the ether," sounds instantly suspect to modern ears, but ether—the invisible, universal substance that acted as the carrier medium for electromagnetic waves—was a perfectly respectable, widely held scientific concept throughout the nineteenth century.[2] Keely claimed he had been working for two years on the influence of sound vibrations on air and water. A particular reaction had released a hitherto undiscovered force. For Keely, the engineering challenge of the century was to design a machine that would run on his etheric energy.

Never a man to do anything by halves, Keely managed to design not one but several such machines. Displaying a penchant for ludicrous terminology that was to remain with him for the rest of his life, he named one the "hydro-pneumatic-pulsating-vacuo engine." Just a year after his discovery of intermolecular ether vibrations, he stumbled on another new power source, a "hitherto unknown gaseous or vaporic substance."

---

2. It was only abandoned upon the publication of Einstein's Special Theory of Relativity in 1905.

In 1874, Keely demonstrated his remarkable machines to a group of wealthy businessmen whom he invited to subscribe to a new corporation, the Keely Motor Company. It must have been an impressive demonstration. Some ten thousand dollars' worth of stock was taken up before the meeting ended. But ten thousand dollars was little more than a trickle compared to the flood of millions that flowed into the coffers of the company over the next six years. Keely continued to produce, and occasionally demonstrate, marvelous machines, but flatly refused to explain the principles behind them—at least not in terms anybody could understand.

By 1880, the Keely Motor Company was a bubble waiting to burst, and burst it did. Shareholders voted to withdraw Keely's stipend. He found himself unable to pay his bills and teetered on the edge of bankruptcy. Then into his life walked Clara Bloomfield-Moore, a woman whose admiration for Keely and his works was matched only by her wealth. She bailed him out of his current financial difficulties and funded him for many years to come.

If Keely learned anything from this brush with ruin, it was never apparent in his subsequent actions. He continued to make grandiose claims about his discoveries, continued to encourage the investment of vast sums in his motor company, and continued his point-blank refusals to explain how anything worked. (On one occasion he was prepared to go to jail rather than reveal the details of his machines, a stance that had him arraigned for contempt of court.) Even Mrs. Bloomfield-Moore tired of his antics eventually. She withdrew her support when an English physicist investigated Keely and issued a wholly unfavorable report.

When Keely died in 1898, investigation of his workshop revealed hidden tubing, trap doors in the floor, and a secret compartment off an anteroom. There was also a two-ton steel sphere buried underneath the main work space. Skeptics rushed to claim that Keely's marvelous machines had never been powered by anything more mysterious than compressed air. In the face of such damning evidence and Keely's own suspicious lifestyle, it is easy to understand *Britannica's* posthumous judgment.

But easy or not, there are reasons why the jury may still be out on John Ernst Worrell Keely. Probably the most important is the question of motive. A superficial examination of Keely's life leaves you with the impression that the millions that flowed into the Keely Motor Company went into his pocket. This was not the case. Keely did spend a great deal of company money, but not on himself. It went on costly custom-made machine parts for his various inventions. Keely himself survived on a relatively modest stipend until disgruntled shareholders cut it off, and on handouts, mainly from Clara Bloomfield-Moore, thereafter. It is also a matter of record that even when faced with bankruptcy, he refused Mrs. Bloomfield-Moore's offer of ten thousand dollars and eventually agreed to accept only half that amount.

Keely lived his life in his workshop where he built some two thousand pieces of machinery. He seldom took a break. This is not the lifestyle of the average conman. In fact it is very difficult to see a financial motive for fraud.

Was there, perhaps, some other motive? Many men are driven not by money, but by a desire for prestige or power. But these motives will not do for Keely either. Clearly he exercised little control over the company that bore his name—he seems to have spent much of his time at odds with the others involved—and his activities brought him no prestige at all. He was accused of fraud during his lifetime almost as often as he has been after his death.

The assumption that his demonstrations were fraudulent is also open to doubt. While the idea that his machines were driven by compressed air has a superficial appeal, various engineers have questioned it. The hidden piping was too narrow a gauge to have coped with the necessary pressures. The steel sphere would have required a noisy compressor; a silent hand pump would never have done. Most important of all, the workshop was not the only site of his demonstrations. At least one was given in the Catskill

Mountains under circumstances that would seem to rule out any possibility of mechanical thimble-rigging. Twelve mining magnates visited Keely in the hope of finding a cheap, efficient way to extract gold. Keely showed them a small, hand-held machine which he touched to several blocks of gold-bearing rock. As he did so, each one disintegrated, leaving its embedded lumps of gold behind. The miners were impressed but cautious and promised funding for an industrial version of Keely's device only if he was prepared to demonstrate it under natural conditions. Keely agreed and repeated his demonstration in the Catskills using a rock face chosen by the miners. His machine drilled a 4.5-foot-diameter tunnel 18 feet long in less than 20 minutes.

The importance of all this is that if Keely really *was* genuine, several of his devices support the Tibetan reports that sound might be used to influence the weight of, or even levitate, solid objects. Keely had an obsession with overcoming gravity. In 1881, he claimed he had invented a secret device to lift heavy weights for a client in California. Like many other engineers of his day, he was interested in the creation of flying machines. But he never envisaged the powered flight with which we are familiar today. Nor did he see the problem in terms of gliding or the wing movements of birds. His approach was a principle he dubbed "vibrational lift" which seems to have involved some sort of sound-generated levitation.

Keely demonstrated "vibrational lift" again and again. In the spring of 1890, he used it to raise a model airship weighing eight pounds but claimed, "An airship of any number of tons weight can, when my system is completed, float off into space with a motion as light as thistledown . . ." The American writer and Theosophist R. Harte described how Keely "introduced a certain force" to an iron cylinder weighing several hundredweights, after which he was able to lift it with one finger. Mrs. Bloomfield-Moore claimed he was able to carry a five-hundred-horsepower engine from one part of his workshop to another with the aid of levitational appliances. A Philadelphia newspaper carried a story attested by an eyewitness named Jefferson Thomas that Keely had levitated a six-thousand-pound metal sphere—possibly the one discovered under his workshop after his death.[3] ⌇

In a more controlled experiment, Keely caused grocer's weights to float in water when he plucked on the strings of a harp-like instrument. In 1893, Jacob Bunn, a vice-president of the Illinois Watch Company, saw Keely set heavy steel balls moving through the air "simply by playing on a peculiar mouth organ." The Boston scientist Alfred H. Plum witnessed Keely drive machinery and cause a two-pound metal sphere to float and sink in water by sounding different notes on a trumpet. ⌇

All this sounds like support for the stories of sonic levitation that have emerged from Tibet, but Keely's reputation remains a problem. Despite an apparent lack of motivation and the other factors mentioned, his actions were undoubtedly suspicious. For a man who claimed to have invented an almost endless stream of incredible devices, he took out precious few patents—an ongoing bone of contention between his shareholders and himself.

Fortunately, the testimony of nineteenth-century witnesses— who *may* have been fooled by the equivalent of clever conjuring—is not the only thing we have to go on when evaluating claims of a sonic technology in ancient Tibet. As I report in *A Secret History of Ancient Egypt* (Piatkus, 2000), the art of sonic levitation seems to be alive and well in Tibet's next-door neighbor India—or at least it was alive and well within living memory.

In 1961, Englishwoman Patricia (Paddy) Slade (now widowed and living near Bath), visited India with her British army husband Peter. During a stay in Poona, they were advised by a friend to see a particularly interesting religious ceremony scheduled to take place in the city.

---

3. Although if so, the eyewitnesses seem to have overestimated the weight.

The ceremony, which was held in the open air, involved a total of eleven white-robed priests and a boulder which Paddy Slade estimated to weigh around forty tons. The priests circled the stone chanting. On the eleventh circuit, the chanting stopped, each priest placed a fingertip on the rock and together they lifted it shoulder high. They held it in the air for a little under half a minute, then set it down again.

To show no trickery was involved, the priests asked for volunteers to repeat the performance. Paddy Slade was among those who stepped forward. With others from among the spectators she circled the stone and chanted. Then came the attempt to lift it.

To her astonishment it rose as easily as it had done for the priests.

If we have to take seriously the Tibetan claims of a sonic technology (as now it seems likely), it is interesting to note that it seems to have survived, at least in some of its aspects, up to the present day. Madame Alexandra David-Neel reports on a meeting with a "master of sound" in a Bön monastery at Tesmon.[4]

Preparations were being made for a ceremony when a disruption occurred. A man who had entered was ordered to leave by the monks and became extremely abusive. The Bön lama picked up a type of ritual bell called a *chang* and used it to produce waves of disharmonious vibrations. The intruder screamed, fell backward, and left hurriedly.

Madame David-Neel followed the man, who claimed that a "snake of fire" had come out of the chang. Others who had witnessed the event said they had seen no snake, but flashes of light had come out of the instrument. Madame David-Neel herself had seen nothing.

Later, when Madame David-Neel asked the Bön lama about the incident, he told her what the witnesses had seen was the power of

---

4. David-Neel, *Bandits, Priests and Demons.*

the spell[5] he had cast with the aid of the chang. He suggested that the sound somehow created shapes and even beings. Interestingly, when he rang the bell again for Madame David-Neel, it was no longer discordant but produced a "melodious carillon" of sound.

Both Bön and Buddhist monasteries make considerable use of sound as part of their spiritual practice. Virtually every surviving temple has its own "orchestra," but the work of that orchestra seems to be something other than the production of music as it is known in the West. Its function is to create specific combinations of sounds as an aid to activities like meditation. Furthermore, there is an intriguing link between sound and the human body. In 1983, a theatrical piece was presented in Holland based on the electronic amplification of various body sounds like a heartbeat and blood flowing within the veins. Among those who attended the performance was the writer and traveller Erik Bruijn, who had spent considerable time studying Tibetan temple practice. He noted at once the striking similarities between the sounds he was hearing and those he had heard in Tibet. By the time the performance was finished, he had concluded that the typical Tibetan temple orchestra was set up to reproduce precisely the sounds generated naturally within the human body.

A ubiquitous element in the sacred sound systems of Tibet is the so-called singing bowl. Although Tibetans have sometimes claimed to travellers that these bowls are simply food vessels, ritual bowls are carefully crafted from seven specific sacred metals and have clear astrological associations.

The metals used are gold, silver, mercury, copper, iron, tin, and lead. Their planetary associations are as follows:

Gold = Sun
Silver = Moon

---

5. The word used was *gzungs*, which denotes a magical formula and carries the sense of something that grips.

Mercury = Mercury
Copper = Venus
Iron = Mars
Tin = Jupiter
Lead = Saturn

When struck with a beater, a bowl of this type emits a ringing sound, but for ceremonial use, Tibetans generally use a wholly different technique. A short wooden baton rubbed around the rim of the bowl quickly coaxes it into producing a continuous harmonic.[6] Using the bowl in this way lends itself to some curious effects. If you add water to the bowl, you can not only influence the harmonic, but create patterns on the water surface. (You may need to add a little dye or sprinkle powder to make these visible.) Some bowls carefully played will cause the water to splash and fountain. With practice, it is even possible to produce the spectacular phenomenon of a standing wave—a column of water held upright by the power of the sound.

But the really interesting thing about the bowls is that the proportions of their seven metals can be varied so that the harmonic they produce differs from bowl to bowl. The variations are not arbitrary. The bowls are in effect "tuned." The reason for this tuning is the Tibetan belief that sound can influence a subtle energy system that forms part of the human body. 5

---

6. The principle is the same as running a moistened finger around the rim of a wine glass, but the sound is considerably less irritating.

4

SUBTLE ENERGIES

According to the tenets of Tibetan medicine, an embryo evolves a complex energy system during its initial eight weeks in the womb. First to develop are the three main channels (*rtsa*) of life energy. The central channel (*dbu-ma*) originates on the top of the head just beneath the soft spot on the skull and runs down through the spine to a space located four fingers-widths below the navel. The right channel (*ro-ma*) branches off from the center just above the eyebrows, then runs parallel to it about an inch or so away until it rejoins the center just below the navel. The left channel (*rkyang-ma*) exactly mirrors the right on the other side of the midline.

While the center channel corresponds in its location to the spinal cord, it is, like the other two, a nonphysical vein of energy invisible to normal sight. Tibetans believe, however, that the channels are discernable to clairvoyant vision and consequently have recorded detailed descriptions of them. The center channel is hollow, luminous, and blue in color, approximately the size of an arrowshaft (approximately one-quarter inch). The side channels are a little thinner, but are also hollow and luminous. They are different colors—red and white—but which is which depends on whether you are male or female. For a boy the right channel is white and the left red. The reverse is the case for a girl.

Once these three major channels are established in the embryo, minor rtsa begin to form to create a network that eventually stretches throughout the entire body. Some Tibetan sources number seventy-two thousand of these minor channels, but this may be more symbolic than actual to simply suggest there are a great many.

Although the three major channels are often visualized as running in straight parallel lines, this is simply a convenience. In actuality, the two side channels intertwine with the central channel at certain important points along their courses. These points are characterized by energy centers which the Tibetans call *khorlo,* a term that translates as "wheel" and exactly corresponds to the more familiar *chakra.* Chakra also means "wheel" (from the Sanskrit) and the term has entered our Western vocabulary to describe a series of subtle vortices in the human aura through which the universal life force is received, transformed, and distributed throughout the body.

Chakras were first mentioned in Hindu yogic literature. The system was adopted and modified in mainstream Buddhism, then further modified in Tibetan lamaist practice. This has led to differing descriptions of the chakras themselves, but the discrepancies may be more a matter of emphasis and approach than any real conflict.

While there are hundreds of minor chakras, the basic Hindu system lists only a few major centers. These are located along the midline of the body and centered on the spinal column. The ro-ma and rkyang-ma channels we have been discussing wrap around them without actually penetrating them.

Although mainstream Western biology staunchly refuses to recognize the chakras, there seems little doubt they actually exist. The Japanese scientist Hiroshi Motoyama decided to test yogic ideas experimentally. Placing his subjects in a lead-lined booth to screen out extraneous radiation, he set out to measure energy levels generated in specific areas of the human body. He found there was indeed a high-frequency energy discharge at the traditional chakra locations, but more significantly, when subjects with meditational experience were asked to "open" a particular chakra (usually a matter of visualization), the energy level increased when compared to that of the control. Interestingly, when one woman was required to open her heart chakra, a photoelectric cell registered increased light levels as well.[1]

To understand the Tibetan chakra system, it is useful to have some grasp of the original Hindu teachings about the seven major chakras. Under clairvoyant observation, each one has the appearance of a multicolored spoked wheel, or, more poetically, a lotus flower. There is the distinct impression that the centers are in movement, perhaps spinning. These impressions have been systematized so that Hindu doctrine asserts each chakra has its own predominant color, number of "petals," and speed of spin or energy vibration. All these factors are influenced by the health of the individual. In sickness, the chakras grow cloudy and their spin slows or becomes irregular.

Over the years, yogis working with the chakras have built up a series of associations with each one. These include specific sounds, geometric shapes, elements, and even letters of the alphabet. Table 4.1 allows you easy access to this chakra information from the original Indian viewpoint.

Although useful, the table is necessarily limited. For example, to state that the root *muladhara* chakra controls the external generative organs does little justice to the far-reaching influence of this center. Through its links with the sacral plexus of the cerebrospinal system, it controls the lower limbs as well. As we proceed upward through the centers, we can see that the influence of each becomes increasingly pervasive.

1. Houston, *The Hero and the Goddess.*

TABLE 4.1—Hindu Chakra System

Chakra	root	sacral	solar plexus	heart	throat	brow	crown
Location	base of spine	4 finger-widths below the navel	at or just above the navel	midway between shoulder blades in center of chest	throat	between the eyebrows	just above the top of the head
Physical	sacral plexus	hypogastric plexus	solar plexus	cardiac plexus	cervic plexus	medulla oblongata	brain/pituitary
Controls	external generative organs	internal organs of reproduction and secretion	digestive system	blood circulation	respiratory system	automatic nervous system	volitional nervous system
Hindu Name	muladhara	svadhisthana	manipurna	anahata	visuddha	ajna	sahasrara
Petals	4	6	10	12	16	96	972
Color	yellow	white	red	gray-blue	white		
Element	earth	water	fire	air	ether		
Sound	lam	vam	ram	yam	ham	ah (short)	om
Shape	square	crescent	triangle	hexagram	circle		

The sacral *svadhisthana* influences the bladder, lower intestine, urinary ducts, and the process of elimination.

The solar plexus *manipurna* influences the stomach, upper intestine, gall bladder, bladder, gall ducts, seminal ducts in a man, liver, kidneys, and spleen. Like the sacral chakra, it exerts influence on the urinary ducts.

The heart *anahata* influences the physical heart and to some extent the lungs, hence blood constituents as well as blood flow.

The throat *visuddha* is the main influence on the lungs and respiratory system in general and also controls the upper limbs.

The brow *ajna* controls the sense organs, having a special relationship with the eyes, ears, nose, tongue, and skin.

The crown *sahasrara* has perhaps the most pervasive influence of all. The universal life force is believed to enter the body through this chakra and is then channelled downward to the other chakras, which transform it into the specific type of energy required for their individual functions. The chakra itself is believed to be of a different order to the others, existing, so to speak, on a higher dimension of reality and forming a link with cosmic consciousness. At a more physical level, its associations with the brain and the mind allow it direct or indirect control of every bodily function.

Even the sounds given in the table are no more than the "central" associated syllable. The chakras are visualized as lotus flowers, each with a specific number of petals. Each petal has its own associated sound. The six-petalled lotus of svadhisthana, for example, has the central sound of "vam," but each petal (energy stream) generates its own harmonic: "bam," "bham," "mam," "yam," "ram," and "lam." Although credited with 972 energy streams, the crown is often thought of as expressing the infinite variety produced by the interaction of all the harmonics of all the petals of all the remaining chakras.[2]

Alongside these root functions, the specific characteristics of each center has led to symbolic associations with Hindu deities and animals. The heart chakra, for example, has a prime characteristic of motion; hence the choice of a deer as its symbol since a deer's most obvious characteristic is its speed.

Alongside the chakra associations with physical processes and symbols are linkages that extend into broad behavior patterns and mental states. The muladhara is the foundation of the instinct

---

2. In actuality, the number of harmonics generated by the crown chakra is not infinite, but it is very large indeed. Assuming the figures given for the energy streams of the other chakras are accurate, I would calculate a total of 4,423,680 crown harmonics.

for self-preservation and what might be called, without negative connotations, your animal nature. The svadhisthana has an influence on general health and well-being. The manipurna is linked to the emotions and often seems to be a factor in trance mediumship. The anahata is associated with higher consciousness and unconditional love. The visuddha is involved with effective communication, creativity, and, curiously enough, some states of expanded consciousness. The ajna relates to intelligence, intuition, psychic powers, and enlightenment. The sahasrara is believed to show the individual's level of spiritual evolution. It is involved in cosmic consciousness and the ultimate states of enlightenment.

From all this you will readily appreciate that the Hindu doctrine of the chakra system is complex indeed. The Tibetan variation is scarcely less so. Apart from terminology, the most obvious difference between the two is that the Tibetans recognize only five major chakras rather than the Hindu seven. In Tibet, the root chakra is known as *sang-na*, the "Secret Place," and combines the svadhisthana and muladhara chakras of Hindu yoga. The Secret Place is concerned with the whole process of reproduction, while the digestive/elimination functions of the svadhisthana tend to be linked with the solar plexus chakra above.

At the opposite end of the scale, the crown and brow chakras are also combined to form a single center called *hdab-ston,* the "Thousand-Petalled Lotus." The merger is interesting since the ajna chakra of the brow relates to the legendary "third eye" widely believed in the East to be the seat of visionary experience. Tibetans, as we shall see, do not subscribe to the prevalent Western idea that visions are necessarily subjective. They believe at least some visionary states represent a direct experience of other levels of reality. Table 4.2 gives basic chakra references from the Tibetan viewpoint.

The chakras are properly seen as aspects—albeit fairly critical aspects—of the main rtsa channels. Figure 4.1 indicates the relationship and interactions among them.

Table 4.2—Tibetan Chakra System

Chakra	genital	navel	heart	throat	head
Location	centered at base of spine between genitals and anus	at navel	center of chest at level of the physical heart	throat	crown of head extending over forehead
Endocrine System	gonads or ovaries	possibly pancreas	adrenals	thyroid	pineal and pituitary
Tibetan Name	Wheel of the Preservation of Happiness	Wheel of Transmutation	Wheel of Phenomena	Wheel of Enjoyment	Wheel of Bliss
Energy Spokes	32	64	8	16	32
Color	green	yellow	blue	red	white
Element	air	earth	water	fire	ether or space
Sound	ha	swa	hum	ah	om
Direction	north	south	east	west	center
Buddha Quality	infallible	origin of jewels	imperturbable	boundless light	making forms visible
Buddha Aspect	activity	quality	mind	speech	whole body
Mentation	concepts	feelings	consciousness	perceptions	forms
Stupidity (Poison)	jealousy	pride	anger	desire	ignorance
Wisdom (Transmuted Poison)	all-accomplishing wisdom	equalizing wisdom	mirror wisdom	discriminating wisdom	absolute wisdom
Animal	bird	horse	elephant	peacock	lion

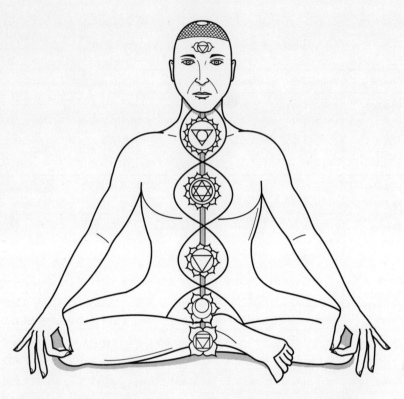

FIGURE 4.1—Major chakras and channels of the human body. In the
Tibetan system, the top two chakras are combined into
one, as are the bottom two.

Some esoteric systems consider the psychic channels and the
energies that flow through them to be much the same thing, but
Tibetan doctrine differentiates between the two. The channels
are clearly described as rtsa, energy courses analogous to a water
pipe, electrical wire, or bed of a river. The energies themselves
are known as rlung, which translates as "airs" or "forces."

A third element in the equation is the *thig-li,*[3] an umbrella
term for certain subtle essences believed to pervade the individual. There are two types of thig-li—relative and absolute. Rela-

---

3. Sometimes transliterated as *thig-le* or even *thigle.*

Chapter 4

tive thig-lis are generated from a single fundamental thig-li in the heart chakra which contains both the essence of the life force and the essence of the five elements. The relative thig-lis are like drops of this central essence which find their way into various parts of the body via the rtsa channels. Tibetan doctrine speaks of a red "mother" drop which moves downward along the central channel and a white "father" drop which moves upward. Relative thig-lis never leave the channels, but having established themselves in their specific locations function as the supports of life and awareness.

The absolute thig-li is quite different. It is neither a drop nor a series of drops and it has no particular location. Instead it pervades every channel, chakra, energy stream, and relative essence throughout the entire system. Lamas think of it as the self-illuminating, changeless, enlightened mind of primordial wisdom, which, unfortunately, goes completely unrecognized in most of us.

Taken together, these three—the rtsa with their chakras, the rlung, and the thig-li—are the major components of a subtle body that interpenetrates the physical and is believed to form the crucial link between it and what Tibetans think of as the dorje,[4] the unchanging "diamond body" that represents an individual's essential Buddha nature or divine spark.

These various elements interact with the physical body and the familiar processes of the mind to form the totality of the human being. From the Tibetan perspective, the physical body depends on the rtsa psychic channels. The rtsa in turn depend on the *rlung,* or energies. The rlung depend on the mind. For a real grasp of Tibetan perspective, it is useful to run this sequence backward. When you do, you realize that the mind (usually by means of generated emotions) controls the body's energies, which

---

4. A confusing use of the term since a dorje is also a ritual implement. The term means "thunderbolt" or "diamond," hence its special usage to describe a subtle body.

control the channels, which control the multitude of processes within the physical body. Thus the mind controls everything— but not necessarily at a conscious level. The Tibetans say the rlung energies are like an untamed horse. The mind is the rider, but the conscious mind has to learn how to get the horse under control.

The mind itself is not entirely what we experience it to be. Tibetan philosophy agrees with Western psychology that there are whole areas of the mind of which we are normally unaware. But the Tibetans go further by postulating subtle levels of mind and mind/energy interactions unsuspected in the West. This brings us back to the concept of absolute thig-li. Although most of us experience our mind as somehow located inside the skull behind the eyes, Tibetans believe the absolute essence of mind pervades the entire body. It is the link with our Buddha nature.

The relationship between mind and the body's subtle energy systems is one of the most interesting aspects of Tibetan doctrine. Speaking at the fourth biennial Mind and Life Conference in Dharamsala, India, in 1992, the Dalai Lama touched on the relationship when he maintained that neither mind nor consciousness were things in themselves, since there were actually many subtle levels and degrees of mind and consciousness. What he referred to as "gross consciousness"—the consciousness we experience in our everyday waking state—depends on the brain for its existence. So long as the brain continues to function, gross consciousness is maintained. Once an individual flat-lines and brain death occurs, the familiar experience of consciousness can no longer arise.

So far, this is in accord with Western neuroscience, but the Dalai Lama then made reference to the idea that a subtle "essence of mind" existed independently of the brain and pervaded the body's energy system, notably at the heart chakra. This meant that from the Tibetan perspective, mind could survive brain death, at least for as long as the energy system remained functioning. In fact, as we shall see, Tibetans accept that a very subtle essence of mind continues to survive even when the entire physical basis of the energy system has ceased to exist—when, that is, the flesh has rotted and the bones have crumbled into dust.

As you will probably have realized by now, Tibetan doctrines of the subtle energies are by no means easy to follow. Furthermore, the variations of the Tibetan chakra system can be confusing to anyone familiar with Hindu teachings on the subject. But an understanding of energy theory is vital to an understanding of Tibetan occult practice, for it is the manipulation of the energy system that underlies almost every spiritual and magical marvel Tibet has ever produced.

MANIPULATING THE ENERGIES

A knowledge of the Tibetan energy system opens up an under-standing of the singing bowls. These bowls are specially—and individually—made to influence one or more of the chakras in a specific way. They are most commonly used in healing and meditation.

I mentioned briefly in the last chapter that the chakras grow cloudy and their spin changes during illness. Although this is true (there is an absolute interaction between the energy systems of the subtle body and the processes of the physical), it is also true to say that certain conditions only influence a particular chakra. If, for example, you are suffering from a heart condition, it is entirely possible this would initially reveal itself solely in the heart chakra. Only after an actual heart attack, which grossly insults the entire body, would you expect reactions in all the major chakras.

The esoteric tradition of Tibet holds there is an astrological component to health and illness. More specifically, the planetary positions in an individual's horoscope show predispositions towards particular complaints. The linkage seems to be energetic; in essence, planetary positions influence the energy system.

There is also, as we have seen, an astrological component to the manufacture of singing bowls. Their constituent metals all have planetary associations. Thus, by varying the relative amount of a particular metal, the bowl can be attuned to a greater or lesser extent toward the associated planet. As you add more copper, for example, you have a bowl with more of a Venus aspect.

Relative metal content is the determining factor in a bowl's harmonic when it is played. Thus, by way of the planetary associations—and, one suspects, centuries of trial and error—a bowl may be attuned to a particular chakra.[1] Bowls might also be attuned to harmonics that would influence more than one chakra simultaneously, or even influence the energy system as a whole.

Unless a bowl is custom made for a particular condition, the likelihood is that it will have a harmonic related to one chakra. When the bowl is sounded, particularly when held at the level of the relevant chakra, it has a strengthening and balancing effect. Some bowls seem to be created for diagnosis rather than treatment. Their harmonic changes as they pass through the chakra system of a patient. A skilled practitioner can listen to the change and determine whether or not a given chakra is functioning efficiently.

In pre-invasion Tibet, singing bowls were even more frequently used in religious and/or meditative practice (the two were much the same) than for healing. In this, they were joined by a host of other instruments, including the human voice. Although the combination of these instruments is often referred to as Tibetan sacred

---

1. Not all singing bowls are made from metal. Rock crystal is sometimes used. Although the direct astrological association is no longer present, careful construction means these bowls, too, can be attuned to a particular chakra.

music, it is not, as noted briefly in chapter 3, music as it is understood in the West. When a Tibetan joined a monastery, usually as a child, sacred "music" became part of his initiation. Typically, the boy would spend his first few years absorbed in menial tasks like serving the salted butter-tea with which Tibetans staved off the cold. But once he was judged worthy, he went through his first (private) initiation, after which he was allowed to play the large drum that beats time at religious ceremonies and processions. This⟩ is a particularly interesting first choice. Unlike most other musical instruments, drums function only to produce rhythms, and certain rhythms have a curious effect on the human mind.

Nerve cells in the brain continually generate electrical impulses that fluctuate in distinct patterns. In 1929, the German psychiatrist Hans Berger embarked on a telepathy experiment that led to his developing the electroencephalograph, an instrument that measures and records brain wave patterns. The recording produced by the instrument is called an electroencephalogram, usually shortened to EEG. The EEG of a normal adult who is conscious and alert shows a predominance of beta waves at 15–30 Hz. As relaxation increases, the brain wave state changes to alpha at 7–14 Hz. Some meditation states are associated with theta at 4–7 Hz, while deep, dreamless sleep is characterized by delta waves of 0.5–4 Hz. But these are only broad subdivisions. Various altered states of consciousness display their own typical brain wave patterns.

Use of the electroencephalograph led to the discovery of a process known as brain wave entrainment. Simply stated, the human brain has a tendency to take on any dominant rhythm in an individual's immediate environment. The rhythm may be visual, audible, or even tactile and is what causes strobe-light epilepsy in susceptible subjects. The reality of entrainment has been established experimentally by monitoring the brain waves of subjects exposed to rhythmic stimuli, but the phenomenon has been known experientially since the dawn of history.

Manipulating the Energies

Voodoo drumming notoriously induces the *loa* possession trance. Shamanic drumming enables the altered states of consciousness needed for spirit world journeys. In culture after culture, rhythmic sound has been used to change human mentation. It seems Tibet is no exception.

But entrainment is no more than the starting point for an immensely sophisticated system of sacred sound developed in Tibetan monasteries. Once the novice has mastered the drum, he learns the long horn, an enormous instrument some three to four yards in length made from copper bound with silver. The horn generates a deep, sonorous, echoing note that can be heard over long distances. After the long horn, the novice will learn the oboe, the conch, and the proper usage of various bells, cymbals, and gongs. Suitable candidates may undergo training in overtone chanting and some are encouraged to develop a deep, raw vocal sound that is quite distinctive to the ear but virtually impossible to describe. Training in this art begins at a very early age—long before puberty—and the style of chanting is considered so important to spiritual development that its practitioners are prepared to risk the destruction of their vocal cords by middle age.

Closely associated with the use of instrumental sound is the practice of mantric chanting. A mantra is a sound, word, or sequence of words used as an aid to concentration. The premier mantra of Tibet is the famous *"Om mani padme hum,"* which translates as "Hail to the Jewel in the Lotus." It evokes a tutelary deity and, according to ancient doctrine, is the essence of all joy, prosperity, and knowledge as well as a major route to liberation.

Like many other effective mantras, this one is circular and is sounded like a snake swallowing its own tail: "Aummm manee padmeh hummm aummm manee padmeh hummm," and so on with the "humm" of the final syllable running into the beginning "aummm." Chanted in this way, the mantra has the effect of stilling the mind by throwing off extraneous thoughts that attempt to intrude into a meditation.

You can experience this for yourself by assuming your favored meditation posture, relaxing your body, and chanting the mantra aloud. Once the circular rhythm is well established you can then internalize the mantra by continuing the chant mentally. If you have not used a mantra before, you will notice at once that intrusive thoughts are minimized when compared to your normal practice. Ϫ

But this is only one function of the mantra. The translation "Hail to the Jewel in the Lotus" points the way to another, even more important function. The clue here is the term "lotus" which refers directly to the chakras. The "jewel" in the chakra is the precious Buddha nature, the state of absolute enlightenment, that Tibetan mystics seek to attain. Thus, the mantra is designed, exactly as the ancient tradition insists, to become a major route to liberation. If you refer back to Table 4.2 on page 43, you will note that the sound associated with the crown chakra, the Wheel of Bliss, is "om," while the sound "hum" is linked to the heart chakra. So the mantra itself combines acoustic structures found over ages of practice to exercise a direct influence on head and heart centers respectively.

Use of the mantra sets up a resonance in crown and heart chakras that eventually refines the entire energy system and does indeed lead to a state of cosmic consciousness. But don't expect a quick fix. The refinement process can take a lifetime, and Tibetans would say several lifetimes. You can, however, test the effectiveness of the sounds by paying close attention to your head and heart centers as you chant the mantra aloud. Almost certainly you will notice an immediate effect at the heart level. An influence on the head center will follow if you persevere.

Energy manipulation is also involved in the training of the lung-gom-pa runners reported by Alexandra David-Neel. She saw her first while travelling through the Chang Thang, a high, grassy region of northern Tibet inhabited by only a few nomadic herdsmen. He appeared as no more than a spot on the distant horizon, but field glasses quickly resolved the image of a lone man moving with extraordinary speed. Madame David-Neel was warned by one of her party that she should not stop the runner or even speak to him, since this would cause the deity which possessed him to depart—something that would shake the man so badly he might die.

As the runner came closer, Madame David-Neel noted his face was impassive and his eyes were focused on a point in the sky. His left hand clutched the material of his robe while his right hand held a phurba. He was moving the ritual dart almost as if it were a staff, although it was not remotely long enough to reach the ground. He did not run in the usual way, but bounded along in regular leaps as if he were a bouncing rubber ball. He did not appear to be aware of Madame David-Neel's party when he reached it.

Later, Madame David-Neel saw another lung-gom-pa in even more curious circumstances. She was walking through a forest in western Tibet with her adopted son Yongden when she came upon a naked man wrapped in heavy chains. He was sitting on a rock and seemed lost in meditation. But then he became aware of them and ran off at astonishing speed. Yongden explained that lung-gom-pas sometimes wore such chains to weigh them down since their disciplines made their bodies so light they were in danger of floating away in the air.

In Kham, that rugged region of Tibet where guerilla fighters gave so much trouble to the invading Chinese, Madame David-Neel met a lung-gom-pa in training. The man joined her party but was with them for a few days before she knew anything about his abilities. Then she saw him climbing a slope with extraordinary speed and agility, using the same bounding motion she had noticed in the other lung-gom-pas. When he reached her, the runner was not at all out of breath, but seemed barely conscious and incapable of speech. She realized at once he was in trance.

Later she learned he had begun to study the techniques in a nearby monastery, but was now in search of a new teacher since his original guru had left the country.

It transpired that the trance state Madame David-Neel witnessed had come on the man spontaneously, triggered by a desire for grilled meat. Although the training methods of a lung-gom-pa were secret, she managed to extract the information that he had been told to look steadily at a starry sky as part of his technique. She also learned that sunset or clear nights were best to practice lung-gom-pa running.

The man was headed for Shalu Gompa Monastery, a center specializing in lung-gom-pa training. According to a tradition dating back to the fourteenth century, the techniques had been developed when a swift runner was needed to collect up various demons scattered around the country. The demons were then propitiated in a powerful and important religious ceremony commemorated at twelve-year intervals right up to the Chinese invasion. A runner, called a *maheketang,* was traditionally elected from one of two monasteries to play the part of the demon-wrangler. His training, isolated in total darkness, took three years and three months to complete.

It is known that maheketang training—generally accepted to be similar to that of a lung-gom-pa—involved breathing exercises and a very curious form of yoga apparently designed to lighten the body. This yoga, reminiscent of a practice that forms part of the modern Transcendental Meditation movement, consists of jumping while cross-legged following a series of deep in-breaths. Since the hands are not used, the knack seems to be related to violent movements of the buttock and/or thigh muscles. But however managed, adepts eventually train themselves to jump to remarkable heights. The legend in Tibet was that after years of practice, the body became so light it was possible to sit on an ear of barley without bending the stalk. In other words, the jumping yoga eventually led to levitation.

Manipulating the Energies

The *lung* of lung-gom-pa is an alternative transliteration of the term *rlung* which describes the energies we examined in chapter 4—a clue to the essential nature of lung-gom-pa training. Indeed, it is known that *lung-gom* is an umbrella term for a series of practices designed to generate physical or spiritual results, of which trance running is only one example. It seems clear that the thrust of the training is an attempt to influence the body's subtle energy system.

Madame David-Neel was so intrigued by what she saw of lung-gom-pa that she made a comprehensive investigation into the methods behind it. She discovered that initial preparation required several years of practice in yoga breathing and only when proficiency was obtained would a lung-gom-pa guru permit a pupil to attempt the actual running. At this point, however, the pupil was given a mantra that was to be recited mentally both in time with the breathing and in time with every step taken.

The running was initially practiced only on clear nights in a fairly featureless, flat environment. This meant the pupil could be assigned a particular star as a focus for his gaze while running. It also meant there were few obstacles to negotiate while he was developing his proficiency. Madame David-Neel records that some runners would stop when their star dropped below the horizon, but others internalized the vision and could continue their journey regardless.[2]

When you put all this information together, it becomes possible to make an intelligent guess about what is going on here. Both yoga breathing and sound have an influence on the rlung energies. While the breath control would almost certainly have followed the traditional techniques developed to strengthen the energy system and promote good health, it is likely that the guru would have chosen a mantra that contained sounds best suited

---

2. David-Neel, *Magic and Mystery in Tibet*.

Chapter 5

to the specific chakra system of the pupil. Although eventually internalized, the mantra would initially have been spoken aloud and the chakras stimulated accordingly.

Mantras are, of course, more than the sounds they contain. A suitable mantra runs to a particular rhythm, and rhythm is hypnotic. But rhythm is not the only hypnotic element in lung-gom-pa training.

A common preliminary to hypnotic induction is to have a subject fix his or her attention on a particular spot above eye level. This quickly has the effect of tiring the eyes and inducing a sensation of relaxation and sleepiness which can be easily transformed into trance in suitable subjects. Exactly the same process is evident in the requirement for the lung-gom-pa runner to fix his gaze on a star.

Another aid to the lung-gom-pa runner's hypnotic induction is the flat, featureless environment. Although this is undoubtedly a safety feature as well, the boredom of running through such an environment is hypnotic in itself. When motorways were first introduced in Europe and Britain, their designers followed the logic of the shortest distance by making them as straight as possible. But there were so many instances of drivers "falling asleep" behind the wheel that artificial curves had to be added. Many drivers did not, in fact, fall asleep at all. They fell into an hypnotic trance.

The fixation of the gaze, the uninteresting environment, and the rhythm of the internalized mantra synchronized with rhythmic breathing and leg movement all combine to become a powerful hypnotic induction. Like early motorway users, the runner drops quickly into trance.

Trance of this type has several interesting implications. As hypnotists have demonstrated again and again, entranced subjects are capable of feats of strength and endurance far beyond anything they might achieve in their waking state. Powers of visualization increase so that the image of the star replaces the actuality and allows the runner to continue his progress during

Manipulating the Energies

daylight hours. So, interestingly, do powers of memory. In Tibet, lung-gom-pa runners were traditionally used as message carriers, yet none of the descriptions in David-Neel's writings or elsewhere mention that they carry scrolls, books, or other texts. The messages, however complex, seem to have been stored in the runner's mind.

Thus the typical lung-gom-pa is a trance runner with a heightened energy system and considerable experience in breath control—three elements that go a long way toward explaining the prodigious feats of speed and endurance that have been reported. But is levitation also a possibility? Many Tibetan texts claim that, in time, a lung-gom-pa may become so proficient that his feet no longer touch the ground.

The demonstrations of "hypnotic" levitation that feature in so many stage conjuring acts are achieved by mechanical means, not trance. But trance can certainly leave you with the subjective impression that your body is lighter, although it is true to say a subjective impression of heaviness is just as likely. If levitation really is a factor in lung-gom-pa running, it is more likely to come about through sonic chanting or some other manipulation of the energy system than simple trance.

Although few Westerners are prepared for the commitment involved in years of training—and indeed trance running through city streets might prove a great deal more dangerous than it ever did on the Tibetan plateau—it is perfectly possible to experience some elements of lung-gom-pa for yourself in your local gym. First, check out your baseline performance on one of the mechanical stamina trainers like the treadmill or fixed bicycle. Then, having rested, repeat the experiment while synchronizing your movements with an inner mantra—you might like to try the famous "Om mani padme hum," but almost any rhythmic form of words will do. You will find your stamina improves. If you can manage to synchronize your breathing too, the improvement can be quite dramatic. Even the simple act of closing your eyes and visualizing a star above and before you can make a difference.

The principles of lung-gom-pa are not the only Tibetan techniques you can test if you are prepared to invest time and effort. Another case in point is body-heat yoga, or tumo.

Tumo adepts were given the title repas (as in Milarepa) after the thin cotton robe they wore in all weathers. Typically, the student of tumo received his repa only after undertaking a rigorous test. Stripped naked, he was wrapped in a blanket that had been soaked in a freezing mountain stream and was required to dry it thoroughly using only his own body heat. When this blanket was dry, he was immediately required to dry another, and then a third. Only after the third blanket was he pronounced proficient in his art. Once qualified, tumo yogis sometimes held contests seated in the high Himalayan snowfields. The winner was the one who melted the widest circle of snow by generating body heat.

The term *tumo* actually means "heat" or "warmth," but only in the special sense of psychic heat. Tibetans recognize three types:

1. The tumo that arises spontaneously during ecstatic religious experience

2. Mystic tumo, which is the fire of bliss itself

3. Esoteric tumo, which keeps the adept physically warm

The third type of tumo—the one with which we are concerned here—is related to the subtle fire that warms the seminal fluid in a man and is the source of its energy (called *shugs* in Tibet). When the warmth is heightened, the energy runs throughout the rtsa channels. Clearly, tumo is not an exclusively masculine prerogative since Madame David-Neel was able to practice it, so the references to seminal fluid in the ancient texts may relate more to a male bias in Tibetan esoteric practice than any technical reality. What seems to be important here is the energy generated at the sexual center, the base chakra Wheel of the Preservation of Happiness. This energy is, of course, common to both men and women.

Tumo initiation is essentially an empowerment, the passing of *angkur* (ability) from guru to *chela* (student). But recognition only comes after a lengthy period of probation and training, so the likelihood is that the chela really does most of the work and the initiation is more to mark a particular level attained than any handing over of a central secret.

In Tibet, trainees were cautioned never to practice inside a house or near other people since "foul air" and "negative vibrations" could hinder progress or even cause harm. Here again is an indication that the practice involved energy manipulation at a subtle level.

Once initiated, the adept was required to renounce the use of fur or wool clothing and never to warm himself at a fire. Like many formalized traditions, this one had practical roots. The practice of tumo requires constant reinforcement. As an athlete who ceases to train soon loses his or her peak level of fitness, so a tumo adept will eventually lose the knack if he relies too much on external heat sources or warm clothes.

Basic tumo training proceeds through three clearly defined stages—preliminary preparation, fundamental practice, and practical application. Each stage in turn has several steps. All three are given in detail in the next chapter.

TUMO

Training yourself in the art of tumo requires a considerable investment of time. In Tibet, traditional training took three years, three months, and three days, and while the period clearly has symbolic associations, mastering the practice in much less than thirty-six months would be difficult for most of us. That said, the various steps of the exercise have benefits in their own right and may usefully be cultivated even by occultists who have no ambition to become a tumo adept. For convenience, the sequence of tumo training drawn from ancient Tibetan texts is here broken down into its component exercises.

STAGE 1: PRELIMINARY EXERCISES
Preliminary Exercise 1: Visualizing the Goddess

In the first of five preliminary exercises, you begin with a prayer to your guru requesting help in the enterprise. The guru-chela relationship in Tibet, as throughout most of the Far East, has implications difficult to understand in the West. It is not simply the association of teacher and pupil, not even that of master and apprentice, although this is closer. It is accepted that the correct transmission of esoteric techniques requires a spiritual bond between the two which involves a telepathic linkage during the guru's life and is sufficiently profound to survive his death. Thus, whether the guru is present or absent, alive or dead, communication with him through prayer is possible in order to obtain his assistance.

This done, you are required to visualize yourself as the naked, virginal, sixteen-year-old Vajra-Yogini, a Tantric divinity who personifies spiritual energy. This goddess has a luminous ruby-red skin and a visible third eye in the middle of her forehead. In her right hand she holds a gleaming curved knife high above her head to cut off completely all intrusive thought processes. In her left hand she holds a blood-filled human skull against her breast. On the head of the goddess is a tiara made from five dried human skulls, while around her neck is a necklace of fifty human heads dripping blood. She wears armbands, wristbands, and anklets, but her only other item of adornment is a Mirror of Karma breastplate held in place by double strings of beads made from human bones that circle her waist and pass over her shoulders. There is a long staff in the crook of her left arm and a flame-like aura around her whole form. The goddess is dancing with her right leg bent and the foot lifted up while her left foot tramples a prostrate human.

Much of this description sounds repulsive to Western ears, but even the worst of the horrors has symbolic significance. The necklace of severed human heads, for example, should be seen as representing separation from the wheel of birth, death, and rebirth that locks humanity into the world of illusion—concepts we shall be examining more fully later in this book.

While the external form of the goddess is as given above, you should imagine yourself internally empty like a silken tent or shaped balloon.

Chapter 6

In your initial visualization, you should see yourself in the form of this goddess about your own size. But once the image is established, you should imagine yourself growing to the size of a house, then the size of a hill. Continue to grow until your goddess form is large enough to encompass the entire universe and spend a little time in contemplation of this state.

Next, you must gradually reduce in size, step by step, little by little, until you are no larger than a mustard seed.[1] Then you should shrink the imaginal visualization still further, so that it is microscopic in extent, yet retains all its fine detail. Contemplate yourself in this minuscule state as well. This completes the first preliminary exercise.

Preliminary Exercise 2: Visualizing the Channels

The second exercise builds on the first in that you begin by imagining yourself as the normal-sized Vajra-Yogini goddess. But having done this, you should now concentrate on visualizing the dbu-ma energy channel that runs down the center of your body. It should be seen as straight, hollow, about the size of an arrow-shaft, and a bright, almost luminous, red.

As before, you are required to expand the visualization until the channel becomes the size of a walking staff, then a pillar, a house, a hill, and finally large enough to contain the whole of the universe. In this form, the channel pervades the whole of your body, right through to the fingertips, although in its natural state it does nothing of the sort.

Again as you did in the first exercise, shrink your visualized image until the hollow channel is no more than one one-hundredth the thickness of a human hair.

---

1. The original texts (notably the *Rdo-rje-hi-lus*) use the Sanskrit term *til,* a tiny seed of an Indian plant. I've taken the liberty of altering this to something with which Western readers might be more familiar.

Preliminary Exercise 3: Posture and Breathing

Your third exercise involves a special posture and breathing sequence preliminary to the visualization exercises. The recommended posture is called the Buddha or Dorje Posture in Tibet and corresponds to the Lotus Pose of hatha yoga. Sit on the floor with your legs crossed so that your feet rest on your thighs, the soles turned upward. Your right leg should be uppermost.

This posture is almost impossible for Westerners without extensive yoga training and seems to have been tricky enough for Tibetans since an easier alternative is given. This is the Siddha Posture—the Perfect Pose of hatha yoga—in which your legs are crossed so that the left heel presses into the perineum while the right foot nestles into the fold of the left leg. The use of a meditation band is recommended. This is a sturdy strip of material roughly four times the circumference of your head, which can be fastened in a loop around the back of the neck and underneath your knees so that it holds your basic posture in place. A well-stuffed meditation cushion about twenty-two inches square and four finger-widths thick is also permitted.

Whichever posture is adopted, you should place your hands in your lap at a level just below your navel with the back bend of the wrists pressed against your thighs. Your thumb, forefinger, and little finger should be extended, and the other two bent into the palm. Straighten your spine and expand your diaphragm as far as it will go. Press your chin against your throat, place your tongue against the roof of your mouth, and fix your eyes on the tip of your nose, the horizon, or the sky.

Once in position, exhale completely to rid your lungs of stale air. Repeat this three times, then inhale as fully as possible and raise your diaphragm slightly so that your chest takes on the appearance of a pot. Hold your breath as long as you can without undue strain.

As you breathe out, imagine that five-color rays emerge from every pore of your body to fill the entire world. The colors, which equate to the elements, are blue, green, red, white, and yellow—symbolizing respectively ether, air, fire, water, and earth. On the in-breath, imagine these rays returning through the pores to feel your body with multicolored light. Repeat the exercise seven times.

Next, imagine that each ray changes into a five-color version of the syllable "hum." This is obviously a great deal easier for someone familiar with the Tibetan alphabet than it is for the majority of Westerners, but a representation of the syllable is shown below for guidance. On your out-breath, visualize the world as filled with these five-color "hum" syllables and listen to the sound they make. On the in-breath, imagine the syllables entering and filling your body. Repeat this breathing/visualization sequence seven times.

Now on the out-breath imagine that the "hum" syllables become mustard-seed-sized representations of angry deities. As a monk in Tibet, you would be surrounded by various representations of wrathful deities, since these have found their way into many religious texts and much religious art. It may be that you will wish to search out and study some of these images for yourself before embarking on this segment of the exercises, but it is an equally valid approach to imagine the deities creatively based on the following description.

First, make no attempt to duplicate the multiheaded and many-armed deities found in some of the Far Eastern pantheons. The gods and goddesses you visualize should have only the requisite single face and two hands. The right hand holds aloft a dorje (see Figure 6.1) while the left is held against the heart. Like the rays,

FIGURE 6.1—Dorje

each deity is five-colored. Their right legs are bent, the left legs held tense. They should be seen as very fierce, angry, and menacing.

Just as before, imagine that on the out-breath the visualized deities go out to fill the world, while on the in-breath they return to fill your body. Again repeat the sequence seven times.

The next step represents a critical stage in the exercise. You are required to imagine that every pore of your body is inhabited by one of these tiny deities with his face turned outward. The result of this visualization, when performed correctly, is that you see yourself as having grown a second protective skin composed of fierce and angry deities, which functions rather like a suit of mail armor.

Preliminary Exercise 4: Visualizing the Letters

You begin the fourth preliminary exercise by visualizing the hollow ro-ma and rkyang-ma channels on either side of the midline. Next you should imagine the five vowels of the alphabet within the left channel and the twenty-one consonants in the right channel.[2] Each letter should have a fine outline and be seen as colored red. Imagine them arranged in a vertical line, one above the other. Establish a breathing routine that alternates left and right nostrils—you may have to close off the alternate nostril with your thumb or forefinger to do this—then visualize the letters streaming out with your out-breath, one after another. On the in-breath, imagine them returning, but entering your body through your penis or vagina. The Tibetan

---

2. Original Tibetan texts state that you should imagine one vowel and one consonant in the left and right channels respectively, but subsequent instructions make it clear that the whole alphabet is to be used.

texts[3] use a particularly pleasing simile for this process: they talk of the letters following each other "like fairy fires." Although the original texts obviously assume the practitioner will be using the Tibetan alphabet, English letters appear to work just as well.

Preliminary Exercise 5: Visualizing the Root Guru

The fifth and final preliminary exercise may present a small problem for Western practitioners. The exercise requires you to visualize your "root guru" seated cross-legged in your heart chakra. The esoteric tradition of the East is based on the concept that anyone embarking on the spiritual path is aided by a series of gurus, many of whom are no longer in incarnation and some of whom are deities with which the student has a special affinity. The root guru, however, is the human teacher seen as the fundamental link to the chain of suprahuman entities guiding the student. A Tibetan will typically identify his guru with no more trouble than you might identify your boss at work, but the West lacks the formal guru-chela structure of the East. Here, as often as not, esoteric knowledge is gained from books, lectures, or group studies rather than one-to-one with a master.

Who, then, is your root guru? The question may require a little intellectual effort to answer. Is there someone, man or woman, who first set you on the esoteric path? Do you have a spiritual adviser? If these questions draw a blank, try thinking of someone who has profoundly influenced you by example—who is, in other words, the sort of person you would like to be, your spiritual role model. Failing all else, you might adopt the author of a book that was seminal in stimulating your esoteric interests.

Unfortunately, identifying your root guru is only the beginning, since the texts require you to visualize the whole succession of discarnate gurus, in ascending order of importance, one above the

---

3. Evans-Wentz, *Tibetan Yoga and Secret Doctrines*.

head of the other in a vertical line along the central channel. In the Tibetan tradition, this chain of spiritual command is clearly defined, with the supreme guru Vajra-Dhara uppermost. For a Westerner who may never have heard of Vajra-Dhara, this will not do. Here again you will need to meditate carefully on those spiritual figures who have most inspired you. For a Christian, this might be some of the saints forming a chain to Christ. For a Jew, it might be the great rabbis or biblical figures like Solomon or Moses. A Moslem chain would extend to the prophet Muhammad, and so on, depending on your spiritual tradition.

Once you have established the chain, you should pray to these gurus using the "Prayer Formula of the Six Doctrines." Here again, problems arise for the Western student since the prayer formula is not some standard text, but rather a form of prayer passed directly to the pupil by his root guru. In the absence of such a gift, you will need to create your own prayer. If you wish to remain true to the spirit of the Tibetan tradition, elements of the prayer might be requests for help with the following: in realizing the illusory nature of reality and the existence of the clear light within, in refining the physical body through yoga and the subtle body through energizing the central channel, and in attaining nirvana and Buddhahood. Since these preliminaries are specifically related to tumo, you should include a request for help in the ignition of the psychic heat.

When the prayer is finished, imagine the entire chain of gurus merging into the body of the root guru which in turn merges into the essence of bliss. Allow this experience of bliss to fill your entire body.

STAGE 2: PSYCHIC HEAT GENERATION

With the completion of these preliminaries, you are now ready to embark on the second stage of tumo, which involves the actual generation of psychic heat. Begin this stage by adopting either the Buddha Posture or Siddha Posture described in Preliminary Exercise 3. (If you have practiced the preliminaries diligently, one of these poses should now be comfortable for you.) In describing the straightening of the spine, the Tibetan texts refer to a column of Chinese coins. The image is particularly appropriate since Chinese coins have a hole in the middle through which the central energy channel can descend.

Once you have adopted your chosen posture with wrists on thighs, tongue touching the roof of the mouth, and gaze fixed on the tip of your nose or the horizon, you should consciously link your thought process with the rhythm of your breathing. The Tibetan secret tradition teaches that your thought processes typically change after a period measured by a single in-breath plus a single out-breath. Control of the mind—a vital aspect of Tibetan esoteric practice—can only be achieved within the constraints of this rhythm. Since breathing and thought processes depend on one another, control of the breath is the first step toward control of the mind.

Breath Control 1: Calm Breathing

The recommended breath control sequence is fairly complex. It begins with the establishment of what the Tibetans call "Calm Breathing" which, in turn, is broken down into two separate parts. The first of these is known as the Nine Bellows Blowings.

Nine Bellows Blowings

Close off your left nostril with your forefinger so that you are breathing only through the right nostril.

Turn your head slowly from right to left while inhaling and exhaling three times through the right nostril.

Now close off your right nostril and inhale/exhale three times while moving your head slowly from left to right.

Finally, with your head steady and looking straight ahead, inhale/exhale three times through both nostrils.

Tumo

This sequence of nine breaths should be repeated three times. For the first of these three sequences, you should breathe so gently that the breaths are scarcely perceptible. For the second, you need to breathe more strongly, while for the third, your breath should empty the lungs completely on exhalation and fill them totally on inhalation. (You will need to make use of your abdominal muscles to achieve this.)

Four Combined Breathing

When you have completed the full sequence of Nine Bellows Blowings, move on to the second element of Calm Breathing which is known as the Four Combined Breathing. For this, you should first bend your head forward so that your neck takes on the shape of a hook. Now draw in air through both nostrils from a distance of about sixteen finger-widths without making a sound.[3] The air from this silent in-breath should reach the bottom of your lungs. Contract your diaphragm to raise the thorax so that your chest puffs out.

You will find this potlike expansion of your chest quickly becomes difficult to sustain. When it does, you are instructed to draw in a series of short breaths using muscular action to direct these inhalations to the right and left lungs respectively so that pressure is equalized in both lungs. Although easy enough to describe, this is less easy to do and may well take a little practice.

Once you have reached your limit in the process of equalization, breathe out through both nostrils gently at first, then with greater force, then gently again, all on a single exhalation. This process is described as "shooting the breath forth like an arrow."[4] When you actually try it, you will understand why.

---

3. This is not a particularly logical instruction, but it communicates well what is needed.

4. Evans-Wentz, *Tibetan Yoga and Secret Doctrines*.

Breath Control 2: Violent Breathing

The second aspect of tumo breath control, Violent Breathing, is another of those practices that can be described a great deal more quickly than they can be mastered. It is broken down into five separate techniques.

The first of these is simply emptying the lungs completely, then slowly refilling them to their fullest extent. The emphasis here is on *slowly*. The stated purpose of the exercise is to prevent the rebound effect—a tendency to take quick, short breaths—which is the natural reaction to emptying the lungs.

W. Y. Evans-Wentz describes the second technique as the "art of inbreathing to cause the air to enter into all its natural channels."[5] No further explanation is given in the original texts, but Evan-Wentz's commentary suggests this simply means working to make the first Violent Breathing exercise habitual. This could well be so, but my own experience of esoteric techniques leads me to believe there may be a little more to it than that. There is a traditional link between breath and spirit (or spiritual energy) that predates every major religion and dates back to the prehistory of shamanic practice. The *pneuma* of ancient Greece could be translated either as "breath" or "spirit." The spirit (life energy) of a dying man in many cultures was believed to leave the body with the last breath. African witch doctors will sometimes breathe spirit energy into a patient to help his or her recovery. The same link is made in the East where the universal life force is believed to be generated in the sun but carried in the air. In view of this and the exercises that follow, I think this second technique should be performed in the conscious knowledge that you are breathing in energy with each breath. Although it appears nowhere in the Tibetan texts, I believe that visualization of the energy as white light will be of benefit here.

---

5. Ibid.

The third technique, known as the Art of Maximum Lung Expansion, is designed to take control of the breath. Almost certainly this refers to breath retention, which permits a fuller extraction of the vital energy from the air. Practice will, of course, enable you to hold your breath for increasingly longer periods of time, but it is important to do so without strain. No yogic practice should leave you red in the face and panting. It is also important to be conscious of the purpose of the exercise—the extraction of vital energy from the retained air. Here too, visualization will be of benefit.

Technique four seeks complete mastery over the breathing process so that the vital energy extracted from the air enters the various rtsa channels. This process, which reflects certain exercises used in the Western Esoteric Tradition, can definitely be aided by visualization. Imagine the light gently spreading throughout your entire body and permeating every pore.

The final technique of the sequence seeks to mingle the internalized life force with the great reservoir of cosmic energy all around you. This is referred to as the Art of Relaxing the Breathing, a name which suggests the process involves an out-breath. The chakras are the centers at which internal and external life energies combine, so a chakra visualization in their relevant colors (see Table 4.2 in chapter 4) may be helpful.

The Mental Images

With the completion of the breathing exercises, we come to the third and final part of the tumo technique. By now it should come as little surprise to learn that it involves the manipulation of mental images.

The first of these is one with which you are already familiar from the preliminary exercises—the image of the Vajra-Yogini. But now, instead of imagining yourself as this deity, you should create an image of the goddess standing at normal human size before you. This image becomes your contact point with the universal energy and part of a visualized "generator" that will produce the psychic heat.

The second visualization is of the central dbu-ma channel with its four major chakras flanked by the ro-ma and rkyang-ma channels on the right and left respectively. Begin by visualizing the hollow, perpendicular central channel, red in color but transparent and bright. This channel, you will recall, begins at the crown of the head and ends four finger-widths below the navel. Next, visualize the two peripheral channels that extend over the top of the brain and pass through the openings of the nostrils to travel downward, flanking the central channel until they curve inward to join it at the bottom. (Refer back to Figure 4.1 in chapter 4 as a guide to the way the side channels interweave with the central channel like a caduceus.)

With the three channels clearly visualized, you should add the chakras to your image. The crown chakra should be visualized as radiating thirty-two "energy spokes"—minor rtsa channels— downward into the head. These are met by sixteen more which radiate upward from the throat center. Eight channels radiate down from the heart center, while sixty-four radiate up from the navel center. The texts suggest that these visualizations are somewhat like the spokes of chariot wheels on the axis of the median channel, but the picture is very approximate.

Now comes what is understood as the core visualization of tumo, and a wholly unexpected one it turns out to be. According to the ancient texts, the secret of producing psychic heat lies in the use of one-half of the letter *A*.

In the preliminary exercises, visualized letters of the alphabet were used to clear the psychic channels. At that stage, I recommended the use of the English language alphabet partly because the wholly unfamiliar symbols of the Tibetan alphabet (which has sixteen vowels and thirty-four consonants) would have created substantial difficulties for Western readers, and partly because it seemed to me that the instinctive associations of one's native alphabet were needed at that point.

But now we are in a different situation. The phrase "one-half of the letter *A*" is difficult to interpret when dealing with the first letter of the English alphabet. What is clearly meant is that a particular shape *like* one-half of the Tibetan *A* may, by its very nature, be expected to have an influence on the energy system.

This is not nearly so peculiar as it sounds. In 1949, a Czech radio engineer named Karel Drbal successfully applied for a Czech patent on a small cardboard model of the Great Pyramid having discovered it sharpened razor blades. It appeared that the shape of the model somehow "collected" a natural energy that influenced the molecular structure of the razor's edge. The pyramid is just one of a series of devices—the majority developed by a Russian named Robert Pavlita—that seem to produce measurable effects by reason of their basic shape.

The Tibetan letter *A* is a symbol written like this: ᢆ. Half of this symbol must be either ᢓ or possibly ᢐ. According to Evans-Wentz, the former shape, somewhat like the Arabic numeral *3*, is known and used by Tibetan mystics, but there is nothing to stop your experimenting with the second option (which looks a little like a long division sign) to discover for yourself which works best.

Whichever you select, the shape should be visualized at the point where the three major channels meet four finger-widths below the navel. See it outlined hair-thin, reddish-brown in color and hot to the touch, floating and undulating. As it moves, the shape makes a sound like the spluttering of a lighted taper.

Next, visualize the Tibetan letter *ham* on the median channel within the crown chakra at the top of your head. The letter, which looks like this, ᢔ, should be visualized as white in color with a single drop of nectar forming on the "tail" at the bottom.

Draw in a breath to bring the life energy into the left and right channels and see them expand in your mind's eye as if they were blown up by the air. Watch the vital force enter the middle channel and travel down to reach the visualized ॐ which fills out from its original outline until it becomes a fully shaped red form. As you breathe out, imagine that the air leaves the median channel in a bluish stream.

Continue this sequence of breathing and visualization until it is well established—that is, until it becomes so easy the various elements seem to occur of their own accord—then change the sequence slightly so that on the in-breath a tiny, pointed flame no more than half a finger-width long flares up from the outlined ॐ. The flame should be upright, bright red in color, and transparent. It should also flicker in such a way that it appears to be spinning. Now, with each in-breath, imagine that the flame rises half a finger-width higher so that by the time you complete eight breathing cycles, it reaches the navel chakra. Two cycles later the flame will have extended into every petal of this center.

Over the next ten breath cycles, the imaginal fire thus kindled moves down to the lower part of your body, filling your lower abdomen, legs, feet, and toes.

In ten further breath cycles, it moves upward in stages, filling your body as far as the heart chakra.

Over the next ten cycles, it reaches the throat chakra, then, with ten more breaths it reaches the Thousand-Petalled Lotus of the crown chakra at the top of your head.

You will recall that you have already established the letter *ham* (ह) within this center. As the imaginal fire reaches this chakra, it slowly dissolves the symbol over the next ten breath cycles into a pearlescent "moon fluid," which spreads to fill the entire lotus.

This moon fluid is the key to the tumo effect. Watch in your mind's eye as it overflows from the Thousand-Petalled Lotus to fill the throat, heart, and navel chakras, then the entire body, each taking ten breath cycles.

The overall sequence of 108 breath cycles constitutes a single tumo course. To become proficient, you will need to repeat six courses over each twenty-four-hour period in the early stage of your training, stopping only for food and sleep. However, the deep breathing aspect of this yoga has the effect of increasing your lung capacity, something that will be quite noticeable after about a month. With increased lung capacity, you will naturally increase your intake of the universal life force. Once this happens, you should reduce the number of repetitions to four.

STAGE 3: TRIGGERING TUMO

With this groundwork completed, you can trigger the tumo heat in one of three ways. The simplest by far is the use of breathing: push the inhaled air to the bottom of your lungs, then contract your diaphragm to expand the chest. The two remaining methods are as follows:

1. While seated in a simple cross-legged position, grasp the underneath of your thighs with your hands. Use your stomach and abdominal muscles to circle the belly area three times to the right and three times to the left while keeping the torso still. (You can prepare for this by first moving the muscles left and right, then gradually building up to a circular movement.) Churn the stomach vigorously by rippling the muscles from top to bottom, then shake your body like a dog that has just come out of the water. While you are doing so, raise yourself a little on your crossed legs, then drop back again onto your cushion, in effect bouncing a little off the floor. Repeat this whole exercise three times, ending with a more vigorous bounce.

2. Visualize yourself as the Vajra-Yogini with the three main channels, the chakras, and the ৬ symbol all visible. Imagine blazing suns in the palms of your hands and the soles of your feet. Bring your hands together and your feet together so that the suns meet. Visualize another sun at the junction of the main channels four finger-widths below the navel. Now rub

together the suns in the palms of your hands and the soles of your feet. When you do so, fire will flare up to strike the sun below the navel, then the ৫ symbol, and will go on to permeate your whole body.[6] On your next out-breath, visualize the psychic heat going out to fill the whole world.

The ancient texts promise that if you perform twenty-one vigorous bounces while engaging in the visualization sequence and repeat the exercise for seven days, you will be able to endure almost any degree of cold while wearing only the thin cotton repa robe.

Test Exercises

Becoming a tumo adept clearly involves a great deal of work. Can we know beforehand that these peculiar Tibetan techniques are actually effective? Fortunately the effectiveness of Tibetan tumo is open to testing—at least to some degree—without embarking on the full training program just outlined. On a cold day you might, for example, try a visualization of fire at the level of your navel. Make this mental image as vivid and realistic as you can while simultaneously relaxing your body as much as possible. My own experience has been that even this simple exercise is enough to create a subjective sensation of warmth.

The effect is stronger if you combine the visualization with rhythmic breathing. In my own experiments, I used two/four breathing to good effect. This is a breathing sequence I learned in the Western Esoteric Tradition. You breathe in to the count of four, hold your breath for the count of two, breathe out to the count of four, then hold your breath out to the count of two.

---

6. You can experience a curious phenomenon at this point in that the fire will often spring up before your mental eye without your actually willing it, something that seems to support Tibetan ideas of a close relationship between the energy system and the visual imagination.

Work on it until the rhythm becomes easy, then visualize the fire at your navel. A useful variation of the exercise involves counting your breath to the beat of your heart. This has the effect of synchronizing the two major body rhythms and again makes the visualization more effective.

There is also a simplified version of the tumo program that may be of interest to those of you with insufficient time to tackle the full thing. In this, you begin by sitting cross-legged in one of two basic yoga meditational postures, Buddha or Siddha, described earlier in this chapter. Begin deep breathing through your nose to clear the nasal passages. Imagine you are breathing out all pride, anger, lust, and other negative emotions, then imagine you are breathing in blessings, Buddha spirit, and wisdom.

Continue the imaginal breathing until you achieve a calm state of mind, then visualize a golden lotus at the level of your navel. Inside the lotus, shining brightly, visualize the Tibetan "hum" symbol for the life force of divine beings:

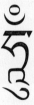

As you watch, the Vajra-Yogini goddess (described at the beginning of this chapter) emerges from the symbol and you merge with her by an effort of imagination. Once you have done so, you should visualize the short letter A, ཨ, in the navel chakra and the letter *ham,* ཧཾ, in the crown.

Take slow, deep breaths to awaken the fire at the navel. These breaths act as a bellows and the fire starts as a tiny ball that gradually gets bigger. The fire then travels along the central channel. You visualize the channel first as a thread filled with fire, but then see it increase to the width of your little finger, then the size of your arm, then filling your whole body with a pillar of fire. Extend the pillar to fill the world.

Hold the picture of the world filled with flame for a moment, then reverse the process of the visualization so that the fire shrinks back to fill your body, then becomes a diminishing pillar, then a thread of flame in the central channel that eventually vanishes.

This simplified version of the tumo exercise will not transform you into an adept, but it may be effective enough to convince you that full tumo training would produce far more dramatic results.

7

REINCARNATION

Traditional Tibet was a culture nurtured in a land of biting cold. Wood was so scarce that animal dung was routinely used for fires. In the worst-hit areas of this vast land, native Tibetans dug themselves underground houses in order to survive the rigors of winter. It is easy to see why such a culture should have taken to a yoga dedicated to the generation of body heat.

It is less easy to see why the Tibetan Esoteric Tradition embraced the rite of *Chöd*. As it is described by Alexandra David-Neel, this macabre ceremony is so dangerous it can sometimes lead to madness or even death.[1] The rite itself is held anywhere that inspires terror—a haunted house or graveyard would be ideal, as would the site of a recent disaster. In Tibet, wild, desolate, barren environments tended to be chosen.

The initiate is equipped with a bell, dorje, the ritual dart known as a phurba, a small damaru drum, and the human

---

1. David-Neel, *Magic and Mystery in Tibet.*

thighbone trumpet called a kangling. After some lengthy preliminaries aimed, among other things, at calming passions, he
evokes a fearsome feminine deity who, if all goes well, emerges
from the top of his head and faces him with a vicious sword in
her hand.

Evocation has been an important aspect of the Western Esoteric Tradition since the Middle Ages, but the entities called are
usually required to aid the conjurer. In this case, however, the
deity is required to cut off the initiate's head. As she does so with
a single swing of her sword, hungry ghouls begin to gather. The
goddess then embarks on a hideous process of butchery. She
removes the initiate's arms and legs, then flays the skin from his
entire body. Next she cuts open his stomach and abdomen so that
his glistening intestines slide out onto the ground. The ghouls
hurl themselves upon the feast.

What on earth is going on here? The grisly rite of Chöd is
deemed to be so important that some lamas used to devote years
to its practice, wandering into India, Nepal, Bhutan, and China
in an effort to find new locations when they had exhausted suitable sites in their native Tibet. One tradition required that it be
performed near 108 lakes and 108 cemeteries. Yet from a Western perspective, it sounds little short of lunacy.

The fact that Chöd can be performed more than once suggests
the butchery does not involve the participant's physical body.
The experience is, in fact, visionary, a trance nightmare voluntarily repeated again and again so that the initiate can feel the
teeth of the ghouls ripping the flesh from his bones and later see
himself as a heap of miserable bones in a sea of mud. But if anything, this seems almost worse than a physical suicide. At least
with suicide you only die once.

To understand Chöd and its immense importance to Tibetan
esoteric thought, you must first come to terms with a pervasive
Tibetan belief touched on earlier: the doctrine of reincarnation.
For while the idea of paying off our debts in a future life sounds

ridiculous to Western ears, there are case studies that suggest reincarnation is a fact of life. One is that of Imad Elawar.

Imad Elawar was born in Lebanon in a remote, primitive village, the sort of place where time stands still and no one travels very far from home. One day he claimed he had lived before as someone named Ibrahim Bouhamzy in a village called Khriby about thirty kilometers away. Although he repeated the claim over and over, his family did not take him seriously—until Imad bumped into somebody he recognized from his past life, a man who actually came from Khriby. Imad's family questioned the man and discovered he once had a neighbor, who was now dead, named Ibrahim Bouhamzy. This gave them the incentive to investigate and they discovered that forty-four of forty-seven items of information given by Imad about the Bouhamzy family were completely accurate, including the fact Ibrahim had had an affair with a woman called Jamile.[2]

How did Imad, in a little isolated Lebanese village, know so much about what was going on in the life of a family thirty kilometers away? The normal information sources like newspapers or tavern gossip can be confidently ruled out. When Imad Elawar started talking about the Bouhamzys and his mistress Jamile, he was only two years old.

There have been similar cases of spontaneous past-life recall from all over the world. Shanti Devi, Bishin Chand, and Reena Gupta in India, Joey Verwey in South Africa, Romy Crees in the United States, and many more are all youngsters who started to recall past lives and gave hard, detailed information that was later checked out and shown to be factually accurate.

Adults have spontaneous recall as well, as a case study from my personal files demonstrates. Some years ago, a woman came to me to ask about a recurring dream. The dream involved crossing an arena that appeared like an ancient amphitheater. It was somewhat

2. Brennan, *Discover Reincarnation*.

like a Roman circus, but smaller and with a friendlier audience. In the dream, she was younger than her current age and dressed in a Greek-style tunic. There was no gladiatorial combat or anything of that sort. She simply walked across the sand, needing for some reason to get to the other side, but awoke before she could do so.

I asked if she was interested in Greek or Roman history but it transpired that she was not. Nor had the symbolism of the dream any particular meaning for her. The only thing she could tell me was that she had first had the dream as a teenager and it had recurred at intervals until her present middle age. It was always vivid and it was always the same.

I had no idea at all why she was having the dream, but the woman was a good hypnotic subject and for that reason I invited her to become involved in a series of reincarnation research experiments I carried out some years later. These experiments used a process known as regression.

The founding father of psychiatry, Sigmund Freud, discovered that many emotional problems were rooted in long-forgotten experiences of childhood. He created his famous psychoanalytical method to help patients recall them. His followers added their own techniques, like hypnosis and narcoanalysis, but all had the same broad aim: to regress patients back to early days and help them remember.

The reality of regression is well established. When regressed to an early age, the subject will typically adopt the limited vocabulary of that age and may even begin to speak in a childlike tone. Personality changes occur. Behavior patterns become those of the suggested age level. If a drawing is requested, it shows a childlike technique. Most interesting of all are the handwriting changes, which often conform precisely to handwriting samples produced by the subject when he or she was actually the age suggested.

In one experiment, a twenty-year-old woman regressed by stages switched the chalk to her left hand when it was suggested she had reached the age of six. She was, it transpired, born left-handed, but forced to switch to her right hand once she entered the educational system. The phenomenon of changed handedness has been seen quite frequently in regression experiments, and has arisen spontaneously in cases where the subject had no conscious memory of ever being left-handed. In such cases, parents or older relatives would usually confirm the regression results. The question of handedness strongly suggests regression subjects are not simply acting out an appropriate part. Another series of experiments has proven this conclusively.

The most spectacular of these involved a thirty-year-old male subject who was seated in a special chair psychologists use to stimulate emotional reaction. (It has a catch that causes it to fall backward abruptly into a horizontal position.) When regressed to the age of one year, the chair was triggered and the man flung back. As an adult, he would have been expected to extend his arms and legs in a reflex compensatory action. In his regressed state, he screamed, fell back, and urinated in his trousers.

At first, psychiatric regressions of this type stopped at childhood. But then in 1898, an enthusiastic practitioner named Albert de Rochas, a French researcher working in Paris, decided to find out if it was possible to regress someone beyond the point of birth. Soon patients were reporting memories of experiences within the womb. Eventually de Rochas made the ultimate jump. His subjects were experimentally regressed *beyond* the womb. Surprisingly, they reported recollections of what appeared to be past lives.

M. de Rochas got little thanks for his discovery. Those in Europe who believed in reincarnation—notably the Theosophists—were interested enough in his work, but found it contradicted their doctrine that the minimum period between incarnations was 1,200 years. (De Rochas's subjects reported coming back in decades.) The British psychiatrist Alexander Cannon brought a little academic respectability to the whole subject. He regressed some 1,400 patients and very gradually came to accept that their past-life memories were genuine.

A few other psychiatrists followed his example, but the profession as a whole quickly abandoned "past-life" regressions as altogether too controversial. The material collected was dismissed as fantasy and the whole episode filed away as an unimportant aberration of the human mind. There were suggestions that pseudomemories of this type were rare, perhaps confined to especially creative patients. My own work gives the lie to that notion. Over three decades, numerous regression experiments have shown that memories of past lives are almost universal.

The question of false memories is more complex. There seems little doubt that some of the "memories" are indeed fantasies created by the subject or drawn from books, plays, or movies long forgotten. But it would be a huge mistake to imagine that all prebirth regression memories fall into this category. Dr. Arthur Guirdham, formerly chief psychiatrist for Bath, England, had one patient who remembered a past life as a Cathar in France. At the time the information emerged, very little was known about this sect and several details given by the woman were held by historians to be inaccurate. But research over the following decade soon established the woman's memory was right and the historians were wrong. The details she had given were verified by subsequent discoveries. It is difficult to see how this sort of data can be dismissed as fantasy.

During the experimental series that involved the woman with the recurring dream, it was my practice to use hypnotic regression to collect the past-life stories, then attempt historical verification at a later stage. Sometimes this verification was forthcoming. More often it was not. There was no way of telling in advance which might prove the case.

During the first regression session, my subject produced a memory of a Victorian incarnation which I found impossible to verify. This was followed by memories of experiences as a nurse on the front during the First World War. The nurse died in the course of her duties when an artillery shell struck her on the back. I was not able to verify this life either, but was interested to note that the woman in question suffered from back problems at the spot where the shell had struck her in the "previous life."

On the third regression session, my subject—who achieved such deep trance levels that she actually relived her memories—reported she was seated beside a swimming pool. Her clothing, a Greek tunic, suggested the ancient world and careful questioning elicited the information that she was a Mede. Her name was Andreas.

Over a period of several months, a comprehensive life story began to emerge. Andreas lived in a city called Xanthus and was the daughter of her country's ruler, Adah. The country itself supported a prosperous maritime civilization, but Adah was under threat from a coalition of provincial governors led by his own brother, Pericles. Unrest developed into open rebellion and Pericles eventually seized the throne. Adah disappeared. Andreas tried to escape, but was captured and imprisoned in an underground cell where she developed a lung condition that had all the symptoms of pneumonia.

While Andreas was fighting the disease, political events were moving in the world outside. Suspicion was growing that Pericles had murdered Adah and possibly Andreas as well. Since the old ruling family had been popular, this was leading to considerable unrest. In an attempt to quash the rumors, Pericles decided to produce Andreas in the public arena to show she was safe and well. (It appeared he could not produce Adah, who had indeed been murdered, almost certainly at Pericles' instigation.)

Men arrived at the underground cell to clean up Andreas and dress her in a fresh tunic. She was certain at the time that she was dying, but when she heard she was to be shown in the arena, she contrived a plan. The judicial system in Media was such that once a formal public accusation was made before the king, the case had to be tried even if it involved the very highest in the land. Andreas decided that if she could stay alive long enough, she might be able to accuse Pericles of her father's murder, thus ensuring he was at least tried for the offense.

With this idea firmly in her mind, Andreas was brought to the arena, and at this point of the story I was confronted with the recurring dream. In the dream, she had been trying to cross an arena, but did not know why and awoke before she could do so. Now, in far-memory trance, she was back in the same arena, but realized she had to cross it in order to accuse her uncle. The story did not have a happy ending. Andreas died before she could make the accusation, leaving Pericles to enjoy his ill-gotten gains.

This was a tale worthy of a novelist—intricate, fascinating, detailed. But when it came to verification, problems arose. Andreas had identified herself as a Mede. There was, indeed, an ancient kingdom of Media in what is now northwest Iran. It corresponded roughly to the modern regions of Azerbaijan, Kurdistan, and parts of Kermanshah. Curiously enough, it was noted for its sophisticated legal system—the Bible refers to the "Laws of the Medes and Persians"—which held that no one, even a king, should be beyond justice. But after that, the story of Andreas parted company with historical reality.

First, it transpired that the capital of Media was not Xanthus but Ecbatana (the modern Hamadan). Nor, so far as I could find, was there *any* city of Xanthus in Media. Furthermore, the country Andreas described had a maritime culture, which suggests easy access to the sea, whereas Media was virtually landlocked. (It did have a short stretch of coastline, but not nearly enough to have developed an exclusively maritime economy.) Historical sources mentioned no King Adah throughout its thousand-year history, nor any King Pericles. There was no rebellion of provincial governors either.

For a while it seemed the whole Andreas story was an elaborate fantasy, but when working to verify far memories of this sort, it is important to double-check the data—and doubly important to make no assumptions. It transpired that one assumption I had made was that if Andreas was a Mede, she must live in Media. Such was not the case.

Although Media began as an independent kingdom, it was eventually dominated by Persia where it played a prominent part in the activities of the Achaemenian Empire. One of the areas of imperial conquest was Lycia, a country that once lay along the Mediterranean coast between Caria and Pamphylia, and extended inland to the Taurus Mountains. This places it in what is now a part of coastal Turkey.

Under Achaemenian Persia, Lycia enjoyed relative freedom but retained a Median ruling class. It was this class to which Andreas belonged, for while I could find no direct historical record of her, the remainder of her story slotted perfectly into place. Lycia was a maritime culture ruled from its capital Xanthus (which lay on the river of the same name) and a satrap (provincial governor) rebellion placed a King Pericles on the throne.

The woman who recalled these memories did not believe in reincarnation. This is by no means unusual. Dr. James Parejeko of Chicago State University carried out a study in 1980 and discovered not only that 93 percent of hypnotized subjects produced past-life recall, but that his best subjects were those who had previously denied any belief in reincarnation.[3]

Against the background of numerous case studies like those of Andreas and Imad Elawar, it seems the Tibetan belief in reincarnation may be very well founded. Dr. Ian Stevenson, a professor of psychiatry at the University of Virginia, has collected more than two thousand verified case studies of reincarnation. He shows that birth marks and other physical blemishes sometimes appear to be "carried over" from one life to the next, exactly as the Tibetans have always claimed.

But recognizing intellectually that the doctrine of reincarnation may have factual roots is still a long way from understanding the emotional dynamics of this fundamental Tibetan belief. For that you really need some personal experience of a past life.

---

3. Ibid.

Fortunately there are a variety of techniques that can bring you such an experience.[4] The first and most obvious is the one I have already mentioned—trance hypnosis.

Hypnosis is a much misunderstood subject. Many people imagine it involves falling asleep, or at least losing consciousness. This is not the case. A competent hypnotist can induce a light trance state in almost anyone without the subject even realizing it. Light trance states are characterized by relaxation and some extremely subtle signs usually only discernable by the hypnotist himself.[5] It is also true to say that light trance is not very useful in stimulating past-life recall. For that you need a medium to deep level of induction.

Statistically, deep-level trance is attainable by only about 10 percent of the population. But medium trance can be induced in over half, so your chances of achieving past-life recall with this method are quite high.[6] Find yourself a reliable hypnotist, preferably one who has some experience of regression. Make absolutely certain you are dealing with someone you can trust. The idea that you cannot be made to do anything morally abhorrent in trance is nonsense. If you happen to be a deep-trance subject, a hypnotist who knows the method can persuade you to do anything he wishes, up to and including murder.

Once an acceptable trance level has been achieved, regression is a simple process. The hypnotist begins by suggesting you return to your last birthday and describe what happened then. Using this as a starting point, he would then typically ask you to

4. For a fuller exploration of the subject than is possible in the present book, see my *Discover Reincarnation* (Aquarian Press, 1992) (first published as *The Reincarnation Workbook*).

5. Hypnotists (and their subjects) may as readily be female as male. I've used the masculine pronoun purely to avoid a tedious use of "he or she" constructions.

6. And they may be even higher than they look. My own experience suggests that factors like a genuine desire to investigate far memory, ready cooperation with the hypnotist, and patience if early attempts fail all combine to make the necessary trance achievable to virtually all those who care to try.

Chapter 7

return to earlier birthdays, perhaps over five- or ten-year intervals, until you are describing a birthday as a child. By this stage, your voice and vocabulary may have changed.

Some hypnotists engaged in reincarnation research will attempt to access memories of the womb at this stage. My own preference was always to avoid it. Birth and death stand as major traumas of reincarnation and I can see no good reason for putting a regression subject through either. Thus my practice was to "speed up" the regression process by taking the subject quickly back through early childhood and babyhood, then "jumping over" the experience of birth/womb/death with the simple suggestion, "You are now going back . . . back . . . back . . . back beyond the point of your birth, back beyond the womb, still further back . . . and now stop."

Once "stop" is called, the question "Where are you now?" is usually enough to elicit a description of a past life, or at least the starting point for such a description. As facilitator of a regression experiment, it is the hypnotist's job to direct the subject in such a way that a lucid picture of the lifetime emerges. This is done by asking questions. Some useful initial questions (on a first regression) might be, "Where are you?", "Who are you?", "What year is it?", "How are you dressed?", "What do you look like?", or "What is your occupation?"

"Where are you?" This is meant to elicit the immediate environs in which the subject finds himself. This is the question one of my subjects answered with "I'm walking along a river bank." Later the hypnotist would try to find out the name of that river, the country through which it flowed, the city, town, or village in which the regressed subject lived, and so on.

"Who are you?" This hopefully gets a name, but not always. In my experiences, a few regressions have taken subjects to cultures so remote and primitive that names were not in use. In such instances, the question will sometimes elicit an occupation—soldier, fisherman, or whatever—or sometimes only blankness.

Reincarnation

92

"What year is it?" Surprisingly, this one can be a minefield. Not all regression subjects belong to a familiar culture in a recent historical period. A past life in China, for example, might result in the date being given as the Year of the Rat. And had it taken place anywhere more than a few thousand years ago, the difficulties will be compounded. Over the sweep of history, humanity has evolved a multitude of ways of subdividing time, not all of them comprehensible to us now. Worse still, some regressed subjects have no interest in dates at all—peasants and primitives will often fall into this category. They follow the seasons because of their importance to agriculture or the movement of game, but outside of that, dates are as alien to them as the surface of Venus.

Should the hypnotist get a confusing answer to this question, he needs to use his ingenuity to establish a rough date some other way. One possible approach is to try to elicit the name of a current ruler—king, queen, emperor, or empress. Another is to hunt for details of recent battles or other broad historical events. If all else fails, fashions in clothing or current technology levels can sometimes give sufficient clues to narrow down the possibilities. (Although you do need to be careful to match technology with culture. Reference to a main gas supply would strike most of us as modern, Victorian at the very earliest. But piped gas was, in fact, available in parts of China as long ago as the fourth century B.C.E. Flush toilets appeared in India even earlier. Like much reincarnation research, establishing even a rough date can be a question of patient detective work.)

"How are you dressed?" This is the sort of question that can sometimes produce important information, but may equally serve only to confuse the picture. Certain styles—the so-called Grecian tunic is a good example—can appear in many cultures at many different times. And what do you do with the information that a regressed subject is not dressed at all? This happened during one of my own experiments and only careful questioning

elicited the fact that I was dealing with a very primitive Egyptian without an apron.

"What do you look like?" This can frequently result in a very vague answer—something by no means confined to reincarnation research since an individual's self-image is often very much at variance with reality. A good hint is to direct a subject's attention to his hands. The hypnotist needs to ask about skin color since the regressed subject will not feel any differently and may forget to mention a pigmentation that can sometimes indicate a broad geographical location.

"What is your occupation?" In some instances, a great deal can be deduced from a subject's occupation. An armorer, for example, fits into a clearly defined time stratum irrespective of culture or geography. Go too far back and no one wore armor. Come too far forward and its use has been abandoned.

Once the hypnotist has a broad picture of the subject's past-life state, he can experiment by bringing the subject backward and forward along the specific lifeline. I often add another question to my original list, "What is your age?", since this gives me an indication of which direction to travel. Once you have an age—even an approximate age—you can fairly quickly decide where the key aspects of the life will be found. Then it is only a matter of careful questioning before an overall picture of the life emerges.

A subject in a medium-level trance will recollect a past life in much the same way you might recall incidents from your childhood: as fragmentary or not-so-fragmentary mental images. Deep-trance subjects, by contrast, will typically relive the memories. This experience can vary from exceptionally vivid mental imagery to something that, for the subject, is temporarily indistinguishable from waking reality. For this reason, deep-trance subjects require careful handling, especially when recalling traumatic incidents.

Although hypnosis can produce spectacular results in the examination and experience of past lives, it is not a technique suited to everyone. Competent hypnotists are not exactly two a penny, and competent hypnotists prepared to devote time to regressions are fewer still. Then too, you may as a subject be unable to achieve a sufficient level of trance for a successful regression. Fortunately there are other, nontrance techniques you can use. Among my favorites is an imaginal exercise I call the Clothing Store.

For this exercise, you need to find a comfortable chair, relax, and visualize the following sequence of events, which may, if you wish, be guided by a friend or even scripted by yourself on a tape recorder:

Imagine you are entering a large department store. As you walk through the door, you realize that all this store sells is clothing—but not just contemporary clothing or regional fashion. As you walk through the store, you can see costumes from every country in the world and every time period you could possibly imagine. Men's, women's, and children's clothes are all stocked, including shoes, gloves, headgear, and accessories.

There is so much clothing in this store that you could not possibly make a reasoned choice about what you want to buy. But fortunately, before you have walked more than a few yards, the owner of the store (a dapper little man with a bald head) bustles up and says, "There you are! I've got the very thing for you. Please follow me."

You follow him through to the back of the store where he leads you into a large fitting room. To the right of the door there is a full-length mirror. Directly ahead is a walk-in wardrobe closed over with a velvet curtain.

"It's just in there!" says the owner of the store. "I'll leave you to try it on."

The owner leaves the fitting room and you draw back the curtain of the wardrobe. Inside is a costume, which, when you try it on, fits you perfectly. You walk to the mirror and look at your reflection.

Simple though it may appear, this is an extremely powerful technique for past-life exploration. Examine your reflection in the imaginal mirror and note any changes that may have occurred since you put on the costume. Have you, for example, changed sex, skin color, race, weight, or height? Check your facial features, the color of your eyes and hair. Almost certainly you will discover that the person looking back at you is not the same person you imagined walking into the store. Examine the costume itself, which could be anything from a loincloth to a crinoline, for any clues it may offer to the country of origin or time period.

This in itself will give you some indication of a particular past life, but only to a very limited degree. To go further, you need to imagine yourself as the person in the mirror. Once you do this you will find that as you step back from your reflection, you are in an environment wholly different from the clothing store. Allow the vision to develop in your mind, and as it does so, try asking yourself some of the questions outlined above in the instructions on hypnosis. Alternatively, you can try the exercise in the company of a friend and have your friend prompt your vision with the questions.

Neither the use of hypnosis nor imaginal techniques like the Clothing Store are any guarantee that the "memories" you generate are genuine. The only way to be certain of this is to take careful note of the experiences that arise, and then, when you have accumulated a body of data, try to check out the details against reliable historical sources. You may find there is much you are unable to verify and some that is outright fantasy. But once the time arrives—as it will if you persevere—when you are able to confirm your experience, you will have gone some way toward achieving a Tibetan mindset in relation to the doctrine of reincarnation. And that is the first step—but only the first—toward understanding the Tibetan fascination with Chöd.

8

DEATH

When I used hypnosis to investigate reincarnation, I would typically instruct a first-time subject to, "Go back beyond the point of your birth . . . back beyond the womb . . . back and further back, back, back . . . and stop." I would then ask, "Where are you now?"

For years this technique resulted in the description of a location or incident in a past life which we could then use as a starting point to explore the life further and eventually progress to other lives. But one day, a subject startled me by replying, "I don't know." For a moment I assumed he simply did not know the name of the place where he had found himself, but when I asked him to describe his surroundings he told me he was in a "dense fog."[1] Try as I might, I could not guide him out of it. Suggestions that he walk forward or back made no difference. Nor, very surprisingly, did suggestions that he move forward or back

---

1. Another subject—a woman—in a similar situation said she was in a "pink mist."

in time during the life he was remembering. The result was always the same featureless fog.

Eventually I realized what was happening and confirmed my intuition with some simple tests. I had managed to guide my subject not to a past life, but to a time *between* past lives. Whatever he had experienced then had left no memory trace. In *The Tibetan Book of the Dead,* there is clear evidence that the mystic lamas have for centuries been aware of the "dense fog" my subject experienced and even knew why the interim period between reincarnations is generally beyond the reach of regression techniques.

The Tibetan Book of the Dead (more properly translated as "The Book of the Great Liberation") seems to have been written toward the end of the eighth century C.E. Oddly enough, the author of the book, Padma Sambhava, was not Tibetan, although he did dictate it to Yeshe Tsogyal, who was.

It is difficult to find much sensible information about Padma Sambhava, whose life is so encrusted with mythology that he is said to have been born as a meteor trailing rainbows from the Land of Bliss. The meteor landed in a lake in what is now Pakistan where it transformed into a giant lotus from which a beautiful boy emerged. This was Padma Sambhava who claimed his mother was Wisdom, his father Compassion, and his country the Dharma of Reality.

Rather more realistically, the adept seems to have been born in India where he established such a saintly reputation that he was invited to visit Tibet by the Emperor Trisong Detsen. The Tibetan culture of the time was extremely aggressive—there was a lengthy period during which Tibetan warlords occupied a conquered China—and the emperor was seeking balance in the establishment of his country's first Buddhist monastery. Padma Sambhava and another Indian named Shantarakshita took charge of the project. Shantarakshita became its abbot, while Padma Sambhava "tamed many Tibetan demons," an expression which may well symbolize the spread of his spiritual teachings.[2]

Among those teachings was the *Great Liberation,* a series of doctrines on death and the afterlife states known as *bardos* ("between"). Padma Sambhava was believed to have special knowledge of the bardos because he could travel through them at will while still very much alive—a legend which, as we shall see, could have been rooted in literal truth.

Although Tibetan Buddhism appeared and spread in the eighth century C.E., there was a pendulum swing in the ninth century that resulted in so much persecution that the new religion was almost strangled at birth. It seems Padma Sambhava anticipated this development and hid several of his most important texts, including the *Great Liberation,* at various locations throughout the country. The *Great Liberation* remained hidden for close to five hundred years before it was rediscovered in the spiritual renaissance of the fourteenth century. It was during this renaissance that the body of Tibetan doctrine on birth, death, and rebirth was developed.

Western science has recently discovered what Tibetans seem to have known for centuries—that death is not an event, but a process. Several minutes after your heart has stopped beating, doctors can still record a mini-electrocardiogram by probing for signals from inside the cardiac cavity. Three hours later, your pupils will still contract violently in reaction to pilocarpine drops exactly as they would in life. Your muscles will still shorten if someone taps them repeatedly. Surgeons can incise a viable graft from the skin tissue anywhere on your body within twenty-four hours. They can achieve a viable bone graft forty-eight hours later, and a viable arterial graft even after seventy-two hours. Clearly life does not cease all at once; cellular death can be long delayed.

Even on the macroscopic level, it has become evident that death is a process. Electrical activity in the brain continues for

---

2. Norbu and Turnbull, *Tibet.*

four minutes or more after the heart stops. There have been cases of revival after hours and even days during which there was no discernable breathing or heartbeat. Although there are telling milestones like *livor mortis* during which gravity pools the blood in the body cavities and *rigor mortis* which causes temporary rigidity of the muscles, it now seems we cannot be absolutely sure of death until the corpse begins to putrify due to bacteriological action.

The Tibetan view of the death process is even more detailed and far more subtle than our own. According to these ancient doctrines, this is what you will experience as you die: First, you will feel weakness and sinking, followed by a melting sensation as your body seems to shrivel. Shapes become indistinct as your vision blurs. It is as if you were looking at the world under water. Everything becomes fluid and unclear.

Next, it will seem as if your body has begun to desiccate, but this is the least of your worries since by now you will be starting to feel numb. Here you have the beginning of a general loss of sensation. Sights and sounds fade as your eyes and ears cease to function. You feel yourself to be surrounded by whirling smoke (the featureless fog experienced by my regression subject). Soon afterward, you begin to feel cold.

At this point the first change in your mental processes becomes evident. You find your thoughts are beginning to dim. You are no longer quite so interested, or even aware, of what is happening to you. Your breathing weakens and your sense of smell fades away. You seem to be surrounded by sparks.

Now your breathing stops altogether. Your tongue seems to be thickening and you no longer taste anything. Even skin sensation—the sense of touch—has gone. You might be living inside a candle flame that is flickering just prior to going out.

In Western terms, you are now clinically dead. Heartbeat has stopped, blood circulation ceased, and the brain flat-lined. But you still retain consciousness (although clearly not of the world around you) and there is still activity, unsuspected by Western science, in the subtle rtsa channels. This is particularly notable in the dbu-ma central channel and in its associated heart chakra.

Although the chatter of your thoughts has dimmed and you have lost sensory perception of the physical world, you retain an awareness of a vast sky illuminated first by moonlight, then by bright-orange sunlight. Both perceptions are illusory. They are your respective interpretations of a pearl-drop of masculine energy sliding down the midline from the crown chakra into the heart, and a red drop of feminine energy rising from the genital chakra to lodge in the heart chakra as well. As these two drops meet, they envelop the consciousness itself and create an awareness unlike anything you experienced during your lifetime, a sort of luminous darkness. At this point you lose consciousness altogether.

Or at least, you experience something more or less equivalent to passing out or falling asleep. But consciousness does not exactly fade away. Instead it undergoes a change. Your awareness passes into what the Tibetans refer to as the "clear light," a mystical form of all-embracing consciousness few of us are likely to have encountered before.

If you refer to Figure 4.1 in chapter 4, you will see how the two side channels twine around the chakras established in the central channel. Tibetans understand them as forming a sort of knot to hold the chakras in place. The knot of your heart chakra was tied at the moment of your conception and firmly maintained throughout your entire life. Now it begins to unravel.

When the knot unravels completely, the last remnant of your consciousness finally departs from your body. Here, from the Tibetan perspective, is the real moment of death, something that has occurred far later than the clinical death detected by Western physicians. Now you are about as dead as you are ever going to get. Unsupported by the processes of your physical body or subtle energy system, your mind has become so tenuous that it is scarcely detectable, even to yourself. Your awareness is so subtle that it has almost ceased.

But this is not the end.

What happens next depends on your level of spiritual evolution. If you have arrived at an understanding of the true nature of reality and developed yourself sufficiently to withstand the experience, you will be able to recognize and abide in the "clear light." Without your physical body and energy system, you have become the quintessence of consciousness and, as such, have become one with the Mind of God that manifests the universe. You have passed beyond the need to reincarnate. You have achieved the enlightenment of Buddhahood. You have reached nirvana.

Although offered, so to speak, at every death, this transcendental experience remains beyond the rest of us. For most, the level of consciousness is so subtle that we never recognize it. We look through it and pass beyond it in utter ignorance of its importance. Although the effort needed to attain nirvana is minimal, it is never made and paradise, once again, is lost. Some see the "clear light" for what it is but pull away from it, fearing the dissolution of the old structures and habit patterns that an acceptance of this level of consciousness entails. In so doing, they condemn themselves to another turn of the reincarnation wheel and the inevitable suffering it entails.

Withdrawal from the "clear light" state, either through ignorance or fear, involves a temporary loss of consciousness. You awaken to darkness—an awareness of darkness—without the slightest suspicion of the prize you have just lost. Your essential self, that divine spark of bodiless consciousness, has begun to rebuild the structures you require to take your place once again in the phenomenal world.

But there are still opportunities to reach nirvana. As you emerge from your brief foray into the "clear light," you become aware of what is going on around you. Your innermost self has built a new body, but it is a tenuous, immaterial body like that of a spirit or a dream. Your senses return so you can now see and hear those gathered around your deathbed. But you cannot communicate with them. You have already forgotten the sensations of your dissolution. It is as if you had a brief period of unconsciousness before emerging from your body like a ghost.

Some people with a strong attachment to the circumstances of their last life become earthbound at this stage. They wander in their ghost body trying vainly to influence events in the physical world. Occasionally their presence impinges on those left behind and the result is a haunting. More often they drift into the dreams of a relative or loved one. But most of us avoid haunting. There is an urge to move on and an experience of unearthly lights and sounds. You are moving into a new realm of postmortem experience more intense and vivid than anything you have known on earth.

But intense and vivid though it is, this is the experience of a dream. According to Tibetan doctrine, both the heavens and the hells of your immediate afterlife are self-created, as are the deities and demons encountered there.

The Tibetan texts chart a period of seven days during which dreams of the deceased are concerned largely with mild, benevolent deities and a further five when the deities become wrathful. You can find graphic descriptions of these deities in the Tibetan texts (notably in any of the excellent English-language translations now available of *The Tibetan Book of the Dead*), but they are of little more than academic interest to a Westerner. The Tibetans knew well that the bardo visions have no objective reality, but represent unconscious projections of the individual's hopes and fears. The shapes they take are culturally conditioned. This means that while Tibetans might be expected to see something very similar to the visions described, Westerners by and large will not. Instead our minds will tend to generate appropriate symbolic figures from our own cultural and/or religious background.[3]

The important thing here is not the figures themselves, nor even what they represent, but the fact they are self-created. *The Tibetan Book of the Dead* is essentially a guide to liberation while in the between-lives state and reiterates again and again that the bardos are illusions projected from the deep mind. If, in the bardo state, you can accept this insight, then you have the possibility of escaping the dream and returning to the "clear light" of primal consciousness. According to Tibetan doctrines, there are those who have achieved this liberation at all stages of the bardo experience. Indeed, it is widely believed that enlightenment is easier there than it ever is while in incarnation.

But it is also true to say that as the bardo experience continues, liberation becomes progressively more difficult since the visions of the final five days are driven by negative patterns and emotions stored up during the last lifetime; and indeed, during the chain of lifetimes that preceded it. If you do not recognize the dream figures as symbols of these patterns—and sometimes even if you do—there is a tendency to run from them in terror, just as many of us are frightened to face up to our imperfections during life. It is this flight, more than any other factor, that ensures a rebirth.

For Tibetans, as for all other Buddhists, the circumstances of rebirth are governed by a process known as *karma,* which must be one of the most misunderstood doctrines in the world. West-

---

3. Some years ago I discussed postmortem memories with a woman who had temporarily died on the operating table. Before she was revived, she met with Jesus who gave her considerable comfort before telling her that her time had not yet come and she was to return to earth. The most interesting thing about the experience was that the woman was not Christian, but Jewish. Since Jews were very much a minority where she lived and most of her friends and acquaintances were Christian, it appears she took the prevailing cultural paradigm as the basis of her postmortem dream rather than her own religious background.

erners tend to interpret karma in the light of Judeo-Christian tradition. There are two biblical references believed to be apposite. The Old Testament Book of Job states, "Even as I have seen, they that plow iniquity, and sow wickedness, reap the same," (4:8). In the New Testament, there appears an even more familiar quotation. Galations 6:7 warns, "Be not deceived; God is not mocked: for whatsoever a man soweth, that shall he also reap."

The idea that we get what we deserve appeals strongly to our innate sense of justice and fair play, but conflicts with observation. It is quite clear that very few people get what they deserve. Fortunes are amassed on foot of deception, lies, double-dealing, and sometimes downright criminal activity. Decent, even saintly, people die lingering, agonizing deaths from cancer. Bad things happen to good people, just as good things happen to bad.

For the devout Christian, the conflict is resolved by evoking the idea of a reward in heaven. The Kingdom of God is closed to the wicked. A Day of Judgment is scheduled to sort the wheat from the chaff. The doctrine of karma is seen as a variation on this theme: justice in heaven is replaced by justice in another incarnation. To the orthodox Christian of today, the idea of reincarnation may be in error (although there is strong evidence early Christians believed in it), but the concept of divine justice remains rock solid.

Even in the East, karma is often seen as a judgment imposed by some supernatural agency as a reward for virtue or punishment for wickedness. Terms like "the Lords of Karma" are taken literally and lives are led warily with a watchful eye out for some supernatural Big Brother.

When I first came upon the doctrine of karma in my early studies of the Eastern Esoteric Tradition, I managed to avoid thinking in terms of a divine judge. But I fell immediately into another error. It seemed to me that if karma existed at all, it did so as the result of some principle of balance inherent in nature. In other words, I saw the mechanism as operating "out there" and triggered by actions I performed for good or ill.

A great many people share this view of karma—the word itself means "action" after all—but it remains just as erroneous as the idea of a supernatural judge. Karma is not a process that operates in nature. It is a process that operates in the human mind.

Karma is not so much action as reaction. Your reaction to any experience, internal or external, leaves a trace on your mind.[4] That mental trace conditions your subsequent reactions, which in turn leave more mental traces, which determine future reactions, and so on. Since your reactions govern your actions, the karmic process, if left unchecked, will determine the course of your life.

Defined in this way, karma becomes more than an interesting theory and can be illustrated by any number of psychological case studies. In the one following drawn from my personal files, the name and identifying circumstances have been changed to protect the individual involved.

Deirdre was a thirty-five-year-old executive in a California company. Her career was going well, but her personal life was in shambles. She was already married and divorced twice, both times to abusive husbands. Since the second divorce, she had had a series of affairs with grossly unsuitable men. One was an alcoholic who became violent when drunk. Another was a drug dealer with Mob connections.

In therapy, it transpired that Deirdre was sexually abused by her father as a child, then beaten to ensure she did not tell any-one about it. She felt guilty about the sexual contact, which she thought was somehow her fault, and believed she deserved the beating. The sexual contact was repeated twice more, then the abuse stopped. Deirdre's father became withdrawn and distant. Deirdre, who still loved him, felt isolated.

In adult life, Deirdre's therapist explained that the childhood experience had set up an unconscious pattern that repeated

---

4. Tibetan lamas would add the proviso that your reaction is driven by aversion or desire, near-universal motivations in the West.

throughout her life. (Prior to her first marriage in her twenties, a series of teenage relationships ended in her being unceremoniously dumped after she slept with the boys concerned, which she tended to do quite early in the relationship.) In effect, she was trying to redeem the emotional loss of her father by attracting a similar type of man with whom, hopefully, she could work something out. Of course she never did work anything out since the whole process was unconscious.

A karmic analysis of Deirdre's situation is not so very different from that of a conventional psychologist. Deirdre reacted, with both aversion *and* desire, to the abuse she experienced as a little girl. Her reaction left a mental trace. When she cast about for a boyfriend after puberty, the karmic trace prompted her to offer him sex (since she had been taught by her father this was what men wanted in return for love), then drove her to become so demanding of affection that the young man—scarcely more than a child himself—ran scared and broke off contact.

Unfortunately but predictably, Deirdre reacted to this development just as strongly as she had to the original abuse, thus laying down more karmic traces that negatively influenced her next teenage relationship, which laid down further traces. Thus karma generated karma in a downward spiral that went a long way toward ruining her life before she had even reached middle age.

Deirdre had a choice about the way she reacted to the circumstances that laid down these traces, if not as a little child, then at any later stage when she repeated the pattern. Indeed, her consultation of a therapist marked a decision to do just that. Deirdre realized that the common denominator in all her failed relationships was herself. If she wanted to do something about the recurring pain in her life, it was herself she had to change, which is another way of saying she had to nullify the karmic traces.

Deirdre's story and others like it show that karma has never functioned, as I once believed, like a cosmic balance that eventually sets things to rights. Deirdre was not, by any stretch of the imagination, a wicked child. She was simply the victim of her father's sexual frustrations. But she paid a price in misery just the same.

In order to understand, and eventually deal with, the realities of karma, it is useful to stop thinking in terms of good and evil and think instead in terms of cause and effect. It is also very useful indeed to remember, and keep remembering, that it is our *reaction* to circumstances and not the circumstances themselves that produces the karmic trace. Together with a developed sense of self-responsibility, these realizations can lay the foundations of a substantially more comfortable future.

Within the sequence of cause and effect, there are certain reactions that are likely to attract unpleasant karmic consequences. Take, for example, the emotion of anger. If something upsets us, we all know how easy it is to react with anger. This is particularly true when we are faced with others' anger. It seems like the most natural thing in the world and there are even (Western) schools of psychological thought that believe it is a bad thing for anger to be suppressed.

Yet anger, even righteous anger, leaves a negative karmic residue. That residue is neither good nor bad in itself. It is simply a reinforced tendency to react with anger. With this predisposition in place, it becomes more likely that you will find yourself in situations where your anger can be expressed. Western psychology sees this as an unconscious searching out of such situations. Tibetan lamas go further, as we shall see presently. But whatever the mechanism, the result is an observable fact. If you know anyone who habitually responds with anger, you will notice they continually find themselves in situations that appear to justify such a response. Miraculously, people who respond mildly do not.

One friend of mine discovered that cultivating an out-of-control anger response enabled her to bully people and get her own way. Unfortunately the karmic traces this laid down have brought her increasingly face-to-face with situations in which the response becomes necessary. As a result she loses friends and suffers increasing emotional isolation.

Historically, the same pattern was followed by Adolf Hitler, the leader of Nazi Germany. Hitler, too, found that flying into an uncontrollable rage cowed those around him and enabled him to push them around. Once he allowed the anger to express itself, the need for more anger became increasingly evident. Toward the end of the Second World War, anger was about all he had left. His karma led him to a lonely, bitter suicide in the garden of his Berlin bunker with his country in ruins around him.

But it is in the process of reincarnation that the action of karma is most evident. For anyone locked into the bardo dream world, rebirth is inevitable and the circumstances of the next life are absolutely determined by the karmic traces the individual has previously laid down.

According to Tibetan doctrines, there are six possible "realms" into which you could be born, each one the result of your pre-dominant karmic trace. These are, in reverse order of comfort, the Hell Realm, the Hungry Ghost Realm, the Animal Realm, the Human Realm, the Demi-God Realm, and the God Realm.

In the Hell Realm there are nine hot and nine cold hells in which you are endlessly tortured to death, revived, then tortured to death again. The root emotion of the Hell Realm is anger, which leads to the loss of self-control and eventually even self-awareness. Once you become trapped by your anger, you become an active participant of the Hell Realm.

The Hungry Ghost Realm is rooted in greed, which is defined as a level of desire that can never be satisfied. Greed is characterized by the habit of looking outward to satisfy our needs, something which Buddhists firmly believe can only be achieved by looking inward. As an inhabitant of the Hungry Ghost Realm, you will typically have an enormous stomach, but a tiny mouth and throat so you can never get enough to eat. Your environment could well be a waterless desert. Hungry ghosts wander a cruel world without the slightest hope of satisfaction, a world generated by the karmic traces left by their lack of generosity.

Ignorance dominates the Animal Realm. It is seeded in a failure to look beyond the level of immediate appearances to find the reality of your own nature and the world around you. This realm is exactly what it sounds like—reincarnation in the body of a beast, wild or domestic, that lives a life of instinct, deprivation, and fear.

The Demi-God Realm is characterized by pride. Its inhabitants, known as *asuras,* live lives of abundance and ease, but have a tendency to go to war very frequently. They fight not only among themselves, but often take on the gods, who invariably win. This generates hurt pride in the asuras, which leads to more wars, more defeats, more hurt pride, more wars, more defeats, and so on, ad infinitum.

At first glance the God Realm seems almost as desirable as nirvana, since to be born there is to lead a long, long life in which all your needs and desires are fulfilled. But the karmic root of the God Realm is the trace left when you allow yourself to be distracted from what is really important by your pursuit of pleasure. Hedonism is certainly attractive, but it is essentially meaningless. The gods themselves are too distracted by their pleasures to seek enlightenment and are thus condemned like the rest of us to the endless cycle of birth, death, and rebirth.

It is difficult to determine from the Tibetan texts whether the Six Realms are to be taken as alternate dimensions of reality or simply symbolic aspects of our familiar human world. Certainly the descriptions *sound* symbolic. The Hell Realm's life of torture followed by death and rebirth mirrors the Buddhist doctrine of life as a reincarnatory wheel of suffering. There can be very few of us who have not met a "Hungry Ghost" who dedicates his or her life to the accumulation of wealth and possessions, yet somehow never has enough. The Animal Realm underlines how easily instinct and ignorance can lead us away from enlightenment, although whether we can literally reincarnate as animals, as many Buddhists believe, remains an open question.[5] Continual preoccupation with war distracts very effectively from the pursuit of liberation, but, conversely, it can be clearly seen how a long life of ease and luxury produces no incentive to change the picture either.

In any case, rebirth in the Human Realm (rooted in the karmic trace of jealousy according to Tibetan teachings) is a matter of personal experience. It is also subject to a surprisingly logical mechanism outlined in *The Tibetan Book of the Dead*.

As you reach the final stages of your dream encounters with the wrathful deities who personify the negative (karmic) aspects of your character, your chances of achieving liberation continue to diminish. Your consciousness moves farther away from its essence as the subtle body you are building grows stronger. Your thoughts, almost inevitably, turn toward the pleasures of physical existence. Although your personal obsessions are karmically determined, there is an underlying drive that is common to all humanity—the libidinous promptings of the life force. Your memories of life in a physical body generate a desire that draws you back into the world of matter. Your fantasies of sexual pleasure ensure your consciousness wanders into the proximity of love-making couples.

The dangers of this proximity are spelled out in a delightfully bawdy Tibetan folktale. A great guru was walking in the countryside with a group of his followers when, without warning, he suddenly seized the pretty young daughter of one of them and tried to make love to her. The girl's father and some friends dragged him away, beat him unconscious, and left him for dead. His followers, appalled by his disgraceful behavior, deserted him except for his most faithful pupil who stayed until he regained consciousness.

---

5. There are few instances of far memories involving animal incarnations, although in one of my regression experiments a subject did report a past life as a gorilla.

"Master, why did you do such a dreadful thing?" cried the pupil.

The great guru climbed to his feet. "Simple," he said. "As I walked through the countryside, I saw with my clairvoyant vision the spirit of my own saintly master floating through the air in search of his next reincarnation. Thus I attempted to make love to the girl in order to provide him with a suitable vehicle for his next life. But the fools stopped me before I could do so and since there were two farm animals copulating in the field we were passing, I fear my saintly master must now reincarnate as a donkey!" Although not meant to be taken seriously, the story does underline a serious point—when the spirit drifts too close to an act of conception, it is drawn into the womb to begin its next life.

STOPPING
THE WHEEL

One day in the 1930s, an American writer named Peter Kelder was sitting on a park bench reading his afternoon paper when an elderly gentleman sat down beside him. They struck up a conversation and the old man turned out to be a retired British army officer and diplomat who had spent much of his time in India.

Colonel Bradford, as Kelder called him, mentioned a strange story he had heard about a particular monastery in Tibet where the lamas had a "fountain of youth" that maintained their energy and vigor long beyond the time they should have died a natural death. The colonel had been gathering information for several years about the location of the monastery and now proposed a trip to Tibet to find it. He asked Kelder if he would like to get involved.

Although Kelder later claimed he believed the colonel was sincere and the story might possibly be true, it is easy to see why he declined the invitation. The idea of people remaining indefinitely young in a remote Tibetan monastery smacks too much of romantic fiction like James Hilton's *Lost Horizon* or H. Rider Haggard's

She, both of which have essentially the same theme. In any case, Kelder wished the colonel well, but told him he would have to go it alone.

Some years passed and Kelder had forgotten the entire incident when out of the blue he received a letter from the colonel. He reported he was on the verge of finding the fountain of youth he had sought so long. There was no return address. Some months later, another letter arrived. This time the colonel claimed he had actually found the fountain of youth and would be bringing it out of Tibet to the United States sometime within the next two months.

Kelder does not record how much of this he took with a pinch of salt, but several weeks later he had a visitor. Although he was announced as Colonel Bradford, the man seemed a total stranger. The colonel Kelder had met four years earlier was a stooped old man in his late sixties who walked with the aid of a cane. The visitor was a much younger man with a vigorous growth of dark hair that showed scarcely a trace of grey. But on closer inspection, Kelder realized this was indeed the colonel; or at least the colonel as he must have been in the prime of his life. Somehow he had managed to turn the clock back and reverse the worst ravages of aging.

When the social preliminaries were over, the colonel explained how he did it. The full story is contained in Kelder's little book *The Eye of Revelation,* first published in 1939,[1] but a précis of the secret he discovered is as follows: The key to the maintenance of youth, like so much of Tibetan occultism, proved to be a manipulation of the chakras. Interestingly, the colonel claimed there is a central chakra at the level of the knees, but this may refer to the more familiar genital chakra, which does lie "at the

---

1. A revised and expanded edition of the work was published under the title *Ancient Secret of the Fountain of Youth* (Harbor Press, 1985). The version I used was published in Britain as *Tibetan Secrets of Youth and Vitality* (Aquarian Press, 1988).

level of the knees" when the practitioner is seated cross-legged. Whatever about this, the location of the chakras does not seem to be critical to the effectiveness of the system.

The system itself involves five physical exercises—Kelder calls them "rites"—that are performed in a steadily progressing sequence. In the first week of your regimen, you perform three of each. In the second week you add two more. For the third week two more are added and so on until you reach a total of twenty-one repetitions of each exercise. This is then maintained permanently on a daily basis, or at the very least three times per week, in order to obtain full benefit.

Two of the exercises are almost identical to hatha yoga postures designed to stretch the muscles and bring flexibility to the spine, but all five are primarily aimed at controlling the "spin" of the chakras so that they function as they would in a twenty-five-year-old. Since Tibetans believe in an absolute interdependence between the physical body and the subtle energy system, benefits in terms of general health and longevity are believed to follow.

But while systems of this type undoubtedly do form part of the Tibetan Esoteric Tradition, it would be fair to say that the main effort of the lamas has been not to prolong their years on earth, but rather to shorten them. Specifically, the Tibetans have for centuries bent their attention toward developing techniques that will stop the wheel of reincarnation and allow them to escape what they consider a life of *khor ba*. The term translates as "suffering" but carries exactly the sense of the more familiar Indian term *sangsara,* which suggests both suffering and the world that causes it are essentially an illusion.

Here at last we come to an understanding of the rite of Chöd. For if the world is an illusion, so, too, are we, and the properly performed Chöd rite helps us to realize it. The rite begins with a familiar visualization in which the participant imagines himself instantaneously transformed into the Goddess of All-Fulfilling Wisdom who, as in tumo practice, expands to fill the entire universe.

Then comes the blowing of a kangling, the human thighbone trumpet. Ostensibly, this is done to call forth the various demons of the place, but since any instrument would serve such a purpose, the use of a human body part takes on a deeper significance. It conveys the essential contempt the magician holds for his physical body.

The yogi then states aloud the purpose of the rite—good magical practice in both Eastern and Western Esoteric Traditions. He claims to be devoting all his thought and energy to the realization that nirvana and sangsara are inseparable. For most of us, this seems quite nonsensical: the ultimate liberation of nirvana is clearly wholly at odds with the karmic delusion of a material world characterized by ignorance, slavery, and suffering. But for the Chöd practitioner, the duality of this belief is itself a subtle trap. Nirvana and samsara are not different states. Ultimately there is, and always has been, only one state, although we are conditioned by experience (and our fears) to believe this is not so. "I am dancing," declares the yogi, "on spiritual beings who personify the self. May I destroy the sangsara view of duality."

The practitioner then calls to his aid various gurus and deities and begins a dance designed to trample down several clearly visualized elemental entities. But at the same time the yogi must recognize these elementals as no more, and no less, than the personifications of hatred, pride, lust, jealousy, and stupidity, which, taken together, comprise the whole of ego consciousness.

The negation of the ego is only the first step of a process. Next comes a much more dramatic, and potentially dangerous, aspect of the rite. For now the magician bends his will toward the realization that his physical body is as unreal as his ego consciousness. "I dedicate as an offering to all the deities here assembled this illusory body which I have held so precious, without the least regard for it." In some versions of the rite, the adept acknowledges that his body has been sustained by the chain of reincarnations of countless living beings whom he slaughtered for food and clothing without regard for their welfare and that the time has come to repay the debt.

After a prayer to his guru, the adept imagines his body, itself the result of karma, to be an enormous, fat, "luscious-looking" corpse. The wrathful goddess (imagined vividly in tumo practice), representative of the magician's own intellect, is then visualized as standing apart from the body, a knife in one hand and a skull in the other. The deity swiftly decapitates the body and transforms the severed head into a skull that she upends to form a giant cauldron supported by three further skulls. She then butchers the corpse and throws the pieces into the cauldron-skull as offerings to the gods.[2]

The magician now begins to repeat the mantras "aum," "ah," "hum," and "ha-ho-hri," the rays of which he must visualize as transforming his body parts into *amrita,* a substance more or less equivalent to the Greek ambrosia that was believed to be the nectar of the gods.

All this is essentially a preparation of the (imagined) body for the culmination of the rite that follows. The yogi next summons the deities, the eight orders of spiritual beings, elementals, and even the hosts of evil spirits, and invites them to approach and appear in any form they wish in order to feast on the body parts in the cauldron-skull. This ghoulish banquet is then visualized as vividly as possible and the adept watches as his body is entirely devoured.

Bizarre though all this may appear to Western eyes, the key to the entire rite is contained in that final sentence. The adept watches while his body disappears, and in so doing, gradually becomes aware that even without his body he still survives. The corpse was an illusion and as such might dissolve like mist in the morning without his suffering the slightest harm. The only reality was mind.

The concept that the only reality is mind has been taken to extremes in the Tibetan tradition. Long ago, Tibetan mystics

2. David-Neel, *Magic and Mystery in Tibet.*

118

developed a technique that makes even the Chöd ceremony seem a little tame. In *Magical Use of Thought Forms* (Llewellyn, 2001), written in collaboration with Dolores Ashcroft-Nowicki, I present a dramatized account of that development, technical details of which I shall enlarge on here.

The technique is reserved for special initiates noted by their gurus as having unusual potential for spiritual development. Typically it is applied only in a one-on-one situation; never when a group is being taught. The typical sequence of events is this: The pupil learns the essentials of the mystic arts from his guru, a process that may take several years. As he becomes more proficient, the amount of help he requires from his guru naturally decreases. Eventually the day arrives when the guru explains there is nothing more he can teach. The pupil must seek a more advanced master. To this end, the guru suggests the pupil should attempt to evoke a yidam.

A yidam is a divine teacher that embodies an aspect of the enlightened mind and is thus held in especial esteem by Tibetans. There are four main types: peaceful, powerful, wrathful, and increasing. Each manifests in its specific form in order to combat particular types of negative forces. The guru recommends the evocation of a powerful yidam since a creature of this type would be able to serve the pupil's needs throughout the remainder of his life. If the pupil agrees, it is usually with some trepidation. Received wisdom has it that the evocation of a yidam is a perilous process and the yidam itself a dangerous entity. The whole thing is taken very seriously indeed.

As a preliminary, the magician studies images of the deity. These are easily found since they illustrate many Tibetan scriptures. The creature itself is a fearsome-looking entity; like many Tibetan deities, it would strike Westerners are more akin to a demon than a god. The study is prolonged and profound. Tibetan pictures of deities are stylized and the smallest detail is often symbolic. The student makes mental notes of everything about the

yidam: skin coloring, clothing, ornaments, what the creature carries. All are important for the operation that is to follow.

The guru next instructs his pupil to find a suitable place for
the evocation. It has to be isolated and remote. Any interruption
could prove disastrous. But it also had to be somewhere the
pupil can stay for long periods of time. The operation cannot be
carried out in a few hours, or even a few days. The guru suggests
his pupil should find a cave, preferably at a high altitude, where
no one is likely to visit.

The choice of high altitude for the site of the operation is not
fortuitous. As we noted earlier, oxygen deprivation influences
mental function and might leave certain individuals more prone
to communications from spirit entities. In any case, the pupil
begins to search for a suitable site and in the fullness of time
discovers one. His guru requires him to stock it with provisions
to tide him over a prolonged stay. But at the same time the provisions are limited, basic, and spartan. It is clear that the time
the pupil spends in his cave will be uncomfortable, chill, and
hungry.

Before anything more happens, the guru teaches his pupil the
art of constructing a *kylkhor*. The term translates as "circle" or
"magic circle" and would seem appropriate to a rite of evocation. Magic circles figure prominently in the Western Esoteric
Tradition. Witchcraft practice includes a nine-foot circle as a
container of power. Ceremonial magicians draw a circle before
they call up spirits. But the similarities with Tibetan practice are
not nearly so close as they might appear.

Since the Middle Ages, Western occultists who embark on the
rare practice of evocation to visible appearance have used two
geometrical figures in tandem: the Triangle of Evocation and the
Circle of Protection. The equilateral triangle is drawn in the north,
usually with a smaller equilateral triangle inside it. The space
between the two triangles is fortified with divine names, lamps are
often set at the points, and an incense burner is sometimes placed

inside the figure. Occasionally a small circle is drawn touching the sides of the inner triangle.

Like the Triangle of Evocation, the Circle of Protection is usually double. It is also usually a good deal bigger. The twin circle is chalked on the floor and, again like the Triangle, is fortified with divine names and various sigils. Bowls of holy (i.e., blessed) water may be set at the cardinal points. The space inside the Circle might contain an altar, an incense burner, and various magical weapons. The space has to be big enough for the magician and one or more assistants as well.

In Western practice, the Circle is never completed until the magician has entered. As the name implies, it is constructed as protection against the spirit entity to be invoked.[3] The entity itself is called up within the confines of the Triangle of Evocation as a secondary security measure. The small circle sometimes enscribed within the Triangle is a third line of defense.

How is all this supposed to work? Western occultists are not the most analytical people in the world and many practicing magicians would meet the question with a blank look or a mumbling nod toward ancient tradition. Their medieval ancestors would have shown no such hesitation. In a more devout age than our own, they would have theorized that the holy names, blessed water, and various sigils formed a conduit for the power of God, which held evoked spirits in check. The spirits themselves were thought of as objective entities, creatures like the magician himself (although of a different order of being) who inhabited an alternate reality until summoned to this one.

Tibetan evocations, as we shall see, are based on a wholly different set of premises, and the kylkhor is a very different structure to the magic circles of the West. As the guru would explain

---

3. In medieval times, such entities were often demonic, but magicians have always had a healthy respect for spirits—good, bad, or neutral—and tend to take protective measures as a matter of course.

to his pupil, the kylkhor is designed to hold the yidam, not the magician. The magician stands outside the magic circle and calls the spirit into manifestation within it. The rationale remains similar to that of the West, however. The kylkhor circle is there to protect the operator. Once evoked, the yidam is supposed to remain safely inside it and leave the magician alone.

The kylkhor itself is a considerably more complex piece of work than the magic circle of the West. It takes the form of something called a *mandala*. The term is Sanskrit and also means "circle," but in Hindu and Buddhist Tantra it is actually a complex symbolic diagram used in sacred rites and as an instrument of meditation. It is widely believed to be a sacred area that functions as a collection point for universal forces and a receptacle for the gods, so you can readily understand its adoption for evocation.

Although mandalas may be painted on paper or cloth, fashioned in bronze, or even built in stone, the mandalic kylkhor uses a very different technique: the unique Tibetan art of sand painting.[4] In a process that can take weeks, even months, to complete, the guru's disciple first clears and cleans a space on the floor of his cave. He then sets about memorizing the names, lengths, and positions of the primary lines that define the basic structure. The lengths involved are relative, not absolute. Mandalas may be constructed to various sizes, but their traditional proportions will always remain the same.

The pupil next begins to practice the technique of sand painting. Since literally millions of grains will be carefully coaxed into place, this is an exacting process. Six primary colors of sand are used—white, black, blue, red, yellow, and green—but four of these (blue, red, yellow, and green) come in dark, medium, and light shades, giving him fourteen hues with which to work. The sands are stored in small, convenient pots and distributed onto the graphic surface

---

4. Called *dul-tson-kyil-khor,* "the mandala circle of colored powders."

by means of a tapered copper tube. The magician fills the tube with a particular color from a pot, closing off the narrow end of the tube with his finger. Then, holding the tube at an angle, he gently strokes it with a rod. The stroking motion causes the tube to vibrate gently and release a thin trickle of sand. With practice, Tibetan monks learn to release as little as a single grain at a time.

Once proficiency has been developed, the pupil sets about constructing a full-scale kylkhor. First, he marks out the major axes and four base lines that will define his kylkhor using chalk strings that have been previously blessed by his guru. Then, working from the center, he begins to painstakingly build up his picture.

It can prove a complex picture indeed. A typical Tibetan mandala consists of an outer enclosure inside which are one or more concentric circles, which in turn surround a square. Lines run from the center to the corners of the square, dividing it into four triangles. In the center five circles contain images of deities, with this pattern reflected in the middle of each triangle. There are four borders. The innermost depicts lotus leaves, the symbol of spiritual rebirth. Outside that is a circle of eight graveyards, which symbolize aspects of cognition. Then comes a circle of diamonds, which stand for illumination. The outermost border is a ring of fire to bar the entry of ignorance.

Clearly, memorizing and reproducing a picture of this complexity requires an impressive proficiency in the art of visualization. But that is only the start. Although parts of this picture involve large areas of color, others comprise lines so fine they are no more than a grain or two of sand in width. The concentration needed to draw such lines is immense. Furthermore, as the pupil begins to stroke the tapered copper tube, it vibrates with a distinctive sound. The sound is hypnotic. After a period of time working on a sand mandala, the artist passes into a state of trance. Only when the pupil masters the concentration, visualization, and trance state necessary to complete a sand mandala perfectly will his guru permit him to proceed with a yidam evocation.

Equipped with his newly developed skills, the pupil makes his way to his high cave and begins the onerous task of constructing the kylkhor. This job alone may well take months. The last sand mandala I saw took weeks, but involved a team of monks working daily on a rotation basis. A lone magician, however skilled, must take far longer. During the whole period he suffers the deprivations of hunger, cold, and total isolation.

When the kylkhor is finished, the guru comes to inspect it. If he is satisfied, the pupil may proceed to the next stage of the operation. If not, the entire diagram is swept out and begun again.

Once the pupil has satisfied his guru that the kylkhor will safely hold the yidam, the invocation itself begins. In the West, this would require an elaborate ritual involving lengthy prayers and conjurations. In Tibet, however, the main element is simple visualization. The pupil is required to seat himself outside the kylkhor and bend his mind toward visualizing the deity so vividly that it appears to be physically present within the magic mandala.

The training of a Western initiate involves this degree of visualization skill, at least in the higher grades, although the object visualized is seldom a deity. Students might typically be asked to visualize a candle flame or a flower held in their hand until they manage a sort of controlled hallucination.[5] Some authorities insist that if done properly, the visualized image can be seen by others. Although this is not strictly relevant to the case of a yidam invocation where the operator typically works alone, Madame Alexandra David-Neel has reported that visualized entities—known as tulpas in Tibet—can indeed become visible to anyone.

How long the Tibetan student remains in his cave until he is able to see the yidam as if physically present is really a matter of personal talent and stamina. Some pupils manage the controlled hallucination sooner than others. But eventually the task is completed.

---

5. See *The Magician, His Training and Work* by W. E. Butler (Aquarian Press, 1963).

The magician can see the yidam large as life and, quite possibly, twice as ugly. When the image stabilizes, he hurries down the mountain to tell his master.

The guru gives him encouragement and a warning. The pupil is congratulated on his progress so far, but warned that simply invoking the deity to visible appearance—which is what he did with his feat of visualization—is not enough. If the entity is to become his teacher, he must be able to hear its words. Now he has to return to the cave and redouble his efforts until the yidam actually speaks to him. He must enter into a dialogue with it so that he can seek its advice.

This aspect of the operation typically takes less time than the initial visualization to visible appearance. Fiction writers—myself included—have often remarked on the tendency of characters to take on a life of their own, saying and doing things the author neither planned nor expected. In the operation we are describing, the magician would first hear the yidam's words in his mind as if the entity were communicating telepathically. He might well begin a dialogue at this stage. A clever student will ask the yidam's advice on how to proceed. With time, effort, and a great deal of concentration, the day will inevitably arrive when the pupil hears the yidam in exactly the same way as he hears his guru.

When he reports this development, the guru again congratulates him, but tells him the operation is still not over. Now that he can hear the words of the deity, he must receive its blessing. In Tibet, a blessing is an energy transfer accomplished by placing both hands on the communicant's forehead. The student must now work in collaboration with the yidam until the creature solidifies. When the blessing is given, the pupil must be able to feel the deity's hands on his head, and he must know the yidam is physically present, solid, and real.

Once again this work can take several weeks or months. Some pupils never manage it, just as some never even manage to see the yidam in the kylkhor. But the successful ones eventually report back to their gurus that the deity is now a living, breathing creature that has manifested fully in the cave.

Here the guru tells him that while an end to his endeavors is clearly in sight, the pupil must achieve one more thing. While he has evoked a teacher of unsurpassed wisdom, the yidam is of little use to him while it remains locked in the kylkhor. It must be persuaded to emerge from the magic circle so that it can accompany the pupil and lend him its strength, powers, blessing, and wisdom throughout the rest of his life.

Tibetan pupils often balk at this stage since they have been culturally conditioned to view the yidam as dangerous as well as useful. But the guru is able to give reassurance. The fact that the yidam has favored the pupil with his conversation and his blessing indicates the pupil has been deemed worthy of the god's assistance. He need have no fear the yidam will ever harm him.

With this encouragement, the pupil returns to his cave and renews his meditative effort. With time he succeeds. The yidam emerges from the kylkhor, takes its place behind the pupil's left shoulder, and agrees to accompany him for the rest of his life.

Many pupils accept this development at face value and spend the remainder of their days guided by a companion few others can see. They do so with the blessing of their gurus who typically assure them they now have access to masters imbued with the very highest degree of wisdom. But a few develop doubts. They are unable to shake off the suspicion that the yidam is not the teaching deity they set out to invoke, but rather an elaborate construction of their own mind with no reality outside it. A doubting student will usually return to his (human) guru and apologetically confess. The guru will send him back to his cave again and again with instructions to pray and meditate until he has rooted out such unworthy thoughts.

Unfortunately, once doubt takes hold, it is very difficult to eradicate. Those failures who begin to harbor suspicions about their yidam seldom regain their pristine innocence. Try as they may, the doubts remain and have again to be confessed to the guru.

"Do you not see the yidam?" the guru asks his pupil, who admits that he does. "Do you not hear him, can you not touch him, do you not feel the energy of his blessing? Is he not as solid and real as the mountains around you?" The student readily agrees that all this is so, yet he is now more convinced than ever that the yidam is a product of his own mind.

And here the guru springs his trap, for it is only the doubters who interest him. He tells the pupil the yidam really *is* no more than the product of his own mind, but in that it is no different to the mountains, the cave, the sands that make up the kylkhor. No different, indeed, to anything in the physical world. All and everything, without exception, is the product of the pupil's mind.

This is the great secret of Tibetan occultism: the realization that the world—all of the world, without exception—is a mental construct. It has no existence outside of the mind that made it. For the mystic, this great truth is the key to liberation from the eternal wheel of birth, death, and rebirth—why return to a world that does not really exist?

The sorcerer, however, sees matters differently.

DREAM WORLDS

In 1999, Hollywood released *The Matrix,* one of the most remark-able movies ever made. It starred Keanu Reeves and was billed as an action sci-fi thriller, but its basic premise was something with which many Tibetans are familiar.

In *The Matrix,* Reeves's character lives normally in a modern American city until he learns his life and everything around him is actually an elaborate illusion. A war between humanity and intelligent machines devastated the planet before the machines won. But the machines needed electrical power and decided to use the remnants of humanity as biological batteries. (Like all living organisms, the human body does indeed produce a small electrical charge.)

To keep humans quiet, their bodies were stored in nutrient tanks and their brains linked to an elaborate computer program designed to generate the illusion that everyone was living a normal life. Since the illusion was fed directly into the cerebral cortex, the dream world (called the matrix) was accepted as physically real by all but a few who managed, with enormous effort, to see through it.

There were two aspects of this movie of enormous interest to occultists. First, the illusory world had its own rules that could not be broken (like the laws of physics), until, that is, you realized your reality was an illusion. Even then, just knowing you were part of an artificial matrix was not enough—you had to feel it, body and soul. This required substantial training. Only then could you perform miracles like catching bullets or leaping safely from tall buildings.

The second aspect of interest arose out of the movie's plotline. Keanu Reeves became part of a small group dedicated to breaking down the matrix and allowing humanity to experience the genuine, if somewhat gruesome, reality behind it. But one member of the group eventually turned traitor. He did a deal with the machines running the matrix, changed sides, and worked to maintain the status quo. His motive was fascinating. He preferred a comfortable life within the illusory matrix than the harsh reality outside it.

If you've read the previous few chapters, you can see the parallels at once. Tibetan Buddhists also believe the solid-seeming world around us is an illusion, albeit one maintained by mind rather than a machine. Like the heroes of *The Matrix,* a small number of them work hard to break through the illusion to the reality beyond, and some have high hopes that all of humanity will eventually realize the way things really are. They are also aware, from bitter personal experience, that simply believing the world to be unreal is not enough to change anything. Rigorous effort and yogic training are both required to break down the conditioning that holds us in our natural "matrix."

Most intriguing of all, Tibetan philosophers have tackled one of the most difficult questions to arise out of the doctrines of Buddhism: if all is illusion, what is the point of morality and correct behavior? Their answer is twofold. First, experience shows that "correct behavior" and "morality" are important in escaping the illusion. Secondly, those of us who remain locked in the unreal world of sangsara have no option but to obey its rules, just as those who failed to recognize the matrix for what it was were forced to function within its rigid program. While the illusion is maintained, we have the choice of generating positive karma and consequently improving the quality of our future life.

Tibetan sorcerers go one step further. Like the characters in *The Matrix*, they prefer the illusory world to the reality beyond (at least for now), but study its mechanics in order to perform miracles. In essence, they believe that if our world is the product of mind, then control of the mind must lead to control of our environment; what is made by mind can be changed by mind.

These are extraordinary ideas and it is valid to ask where they came from. While we are at it, we might also ask where Tibetan mystics obtained such detailed information about the after-death bardo states and the subtle body energies that underpin such practices as lung-gom-pa or tumo. The answer lies in the country's history. Today, the people of Tibet have earned an international reputation as the most gentle, spiritually evolved nation in the world. It was not always so. For centuries, Tibet produced warlords who were among the most brutal and aggressive in Asia. The Chinese annexation of Tibet in 1950 is mirrored by more than one Tibetan annexation of Chinese territory in earlier eras.

But all that changed with the coming of Buddhism. For some reason, the gentle philosophy of Prince Gautama struck a sympathetic chord in the Tibetan soul. His central precept—work out your own salvation with diligence—was taken up in Tibet to an extraordinary degree. Generations of Tibetan lamas, mystics, hermits, and magicians embarked on an investigation of the human mind unmatched anywhere on Earth. Personal experience was everything. They became "psychonauts" exploring the deepest reaches of inner space.

Among the Tibetans' most intriguing tools was the practice of dream yoga. Although a great many people believe they seldom, if ever, dream, this self-perception is inaccurate. Everyone dreams—as do all mammals, birds, and even some lizards—every night, except in cases of high fever. Although, not everyone remembers; if you are between the ages of ten and sixty-five, approximately a quarter of your sleep is spent dreaming. If you are older or younger, your dreaming time increases.

Over the last twenty-five years there has been a great deal of scientific research into sleep and dreaming. Subjects have been persuaded to sleep in the laboratory wired up to various monitoring devices that measure brain waves, blood pressure, heart rate, and so on. They have been pinched or had water thrown on them. Loud noises were introduced, all to see what would happen. What does happen in a typical night's sleep is this: First there is a transitional phase between the waking state and sleep. Thoughts become hazy, and you react less to external stimulation. This is known as the hypnagogic state, something now known to be conducive to brief hallucinatory experiences (notably voices), and psi activity.

After about five minutes you move to stage two, and the EEG (electroencephalogram) that monitors your brain electricity shows a pattern called sleep spindles. These appear as sharp spikes on the graph.

Then comes a third stage known as delta sleep. Your brain shows a pattern of delta waves, which are slower and larger than the waves characterizing the preceding stages. After some time in stage three, you usually return to stage two for a while.

Now, about ninety minutes after falling asleep, you hit what is called REM sleep. REM sleep was discovered in 1953 when sleep scientists noticed that, about an hour and a half after falling asleep, laboratory subjects tended to experience a burst of rapid eye movement (REM) under their closed lids. This was accompanied by a change in brain wave activity. Curiously, the pattern reverted to that of an alert, awake person. When subjects were awakened during REM sleep, they reported vivid dreams twenty out of twenty-seven times. (By contrast, only four out of twenty-three subjects said they were dreaming when wakened from non-

REM sleep.) The scientists concluded there was a connection between REM and dreaming, something now confirmed by several thousand experimental studies.

(This is not to say you *only* dream during REM sleep. Research has shown that vivid visual dreams are associated with REM about 80 percent of the time. But even without REM, somewhere between 30 percent and 50 percent of wakened subjects reported some sort of dream activity. But since they reported this activity as "thought-like" and "similar to being awake," the experience might be better described as some form of sleeping mentation, perhaps even a paradoxical "sleeping consciousness," rather than an actual dream.)[1]

During dreaming, your brain activity is not at all like the rest of your sleeping state. In many ways it looks as if you are actually awake. Your muscles are extremely relaxed at this time. Usually your first dream of the night only lasts five to ten minutes, after which you go back to stage two—the spindle stage—before returning to another short dream. This cycle of stage two and dreaming alternates over seventy- to ninety-minute periods for the rest of the night.

If you are in good health, you'll normally have about four dream periods every night. The length of each gradually increases through the night, and most of the latter part of a night's sleep is spent dreaming. While you do, various hormone and body chemical levels change. Your brain temperature increases and your breathing gets faster. Although dreams actually occur in color, they often fade to black and white when you remember them.

External stimuli such as a spray of water do not initiate dreaming, although they are often incorporated into ongoing dreams. Most drugs, including alcohol, suppress dreaming. Following a period of decreased dreaming, there is a rebound effect. You get longer dreams more often that sometimes even extend into other

1. *Encyclopedia Britannica,* 1998 electronic edition, s. v. "Dream."

sleep stages. Dreaming actually seems to be a biological necessity. If you are deprived of it for long enough, you start showing signs of psychosis.

You do not dream at the same rate throughout your life. As a baby, you dreamed about half of your whole sleep time. When you grew up, this dropped to something like a quarter—somewhere between a fifth and a quarter to be exact. Beyond the age of sixty-five, there is a slight increase in your dreaming time, although you never revert to the high dream rate of childhood.

Western neurophysiologists tend to think of dream activity as a more or less random stimulation of the cerebral cortex by a region in the brainstem called the *pontine tegmentum*. Dream activity, in their view, becomes an effort by the higher brain centers to make sense of these random stimulations during sleep.

Other researchers have suggested a computerlike function to the dreaming process, comparing it to a program inspection procedure that attempts to integrate new experiences with older, stored memories in the brain. Some theorists have even proposed that dreams are the brain's attempt to rid itself of "bad," accidental connections between brain cells.

But ideas like these are very new. In the ancient world, most people believed that dreams were sent by the gods, and could be used to predict the future, devise medical cures, and receive information. Because of this, they tended to be taken seriously. The Bible reports that a great famine in Egypt was revealed in a dream of the pharaoh, as interpreted by Joseph. (The Egyptians actually systemized the interpretation of dreams, as shown by a four-thousand-year-old papyrus in the Chester Beattie Collection.) Pilate's wife advised him to have nothing to do with the conviction of Christ because of a dream. Cecilia Metella, the wife of a consul, had a dream that convinced the Roman Senate they should order the rebuilding of a temple to Juno Sospita. Emperor Marcian dreamed he saw the bow of Attila the Hun break on the same night Attila died. Plutarch records how Emperor Augustus was persuaded to leave his tent by a dream, even though he was ill at the time. A few hours later, his bed was pierced by enemy swords. Croesus saw his son killed in a dream. Calpurnia tried to warn her husband, Julius Caesar, about his impending assassination because of a dream.

But important dreams were not confined to the great and powerful. The Roman writer Cicero records how two travelling Arcadians went to different lodgings one night—one to an inn, the other to a private house. During the night the traveller who lodged in the house dreamed that his friend needed help. He awoke, but decided not to take the dream seriously and went back to sleep. He dreamed again and his friend appeared claiming he had been murdered and his body hidden under manure in a cart. According to Cicero, the cart and the body were afterward found.

Far-fetched though these reports may sound, there is some reason to believe we should take them just as seriously as current theories about random stimulation of the cortex. In a paper published in the *Journal of the American Society for Psychical Research*, Dr. Mary S. Stowell described how she analyzed fifty-one apparently precognitive dreams and discovered thirty-seven of them were subsequently confirmed as accurate—well beyond any question of coincidence or chance. One dreamer witnessed a plane crash in a specific location, told her husband about the dream the following morning, then watched news reports of the same crash in the same place just a few weeks later.[2]

Even without the element of prediction, dreams have been shown to be far more useful than one would expect from the random firing of neurons. In 1948, for example, the American anthropologist Dr. Kilton Stewart published a paper titled *Dream Theory in Malaya* that described his encounter in 1935 with a native peninsular people called the Senoi.

2. Stowell, "Precognitive Dreams: A Phenomenological Study," 163. Quoted in Corless, *Science Frontiers*.

The Senoi are not only found on the Malay Peninsula but also along the coastal plains of eastern Sumatra in Indonesia. Approximately eighteen thousand of them are alive today following a way of life that combines the cultivation of rice and manioc with ancient hunter-gatherer techniques using blowguns and poisoned darts. They are a primitive people, incapable of metalwork or weaving (except for baskets), yet Dr. Stewart claimed they had developed a system of psychology so astonishing it might have come from another planet. He believed this system was largely responsible for the fact that as a people the Senoi had been free from violent crime and mental disease for more than two hundred years.

(They had also, he said, been free from war for a similar period, but this seemed largely due to their fearsome reputation as magicians. Although the Senoi did not, in fact, practice destructive magic, they permitted other tribes in the region to believe they were perfectly capable of doing so if attacked. As a result they were left alone. The stability of their own culture meant they had no interest in attacking anybody else.)

The system itself, as Dr. Stewart translated it into Western terminology, was based on the idea that all of us create personifications of the outside world in our mind as part of the adaptive process to life. But some of these images are in conflict with us and, indeed, with each other. When they are internalized, the hostility inherent in such images tends to turn us against ourselves and/or others.

In dreams, however, it becomes possible to view these psychic facts directly. The hostile personifications appear as images of other people, animals, nightmare monsters, and so on. Left alone, they interact throughout an individual's life, conditioning his or her responses and psychology until some degree of antisocial behavior is almost inevitable. The images dissociate from the central personality and become tied into emotional stresses and muscular tensions. But the Senoi do not leave them alone. Guided by the insights of medicine men known as Tohats, they long ago embarked on a process of dream interpretation in which the psychological replicas could be redirected and reorganized in such a way as to aid the central personality rather than conflict with it.

Dr. Stewart reported that the Senoi firmly believed anyone, with a little help from his friends, could outface, overcome, and ultimately use all the manifestations of the dream universe. They had also concluded, on the basis of long experience, that goodwill shown toward others during the waking hours ensured help from their images in dreams. To a Senoi, the ideal was complete mastery of the spiritual (i.e., dream) world, something that gave the individual an absolute right to demand help and cooperation from anything found there.

Although the Tohats of the tribe specialized in trance states like those of shamans in many other cultures, dream analysis was carried out by everyone. It became, in effect, a regular feature of tribal life. Stewart described breakfast time in a typical Senoi household as akin to a dream clinic. Children were encouraged to describe the dreams they had had the previous night. When they did so, their father and older brothers (dream analysis was apparently a male prerogative) would listen carefully, explain the nature of each dream, and give helpful advice. These family sessions were followed by more formal tribal councils, again on a daily basis, in which the dreams of the adults and older children were communally discussed.

As an example of Senoi analysis, Stewart mentions a common nightmare—the dream of falling. Reports of such a dream by, for example, a Senoi boy would be met with enthusiasm and the child would be told this was one of the best dreams he could have. He would be asked where he fell to and what he discovered there.

If, as seems likely, the child replied that the dream did not feel wonderful or that he had woken up in a panic before he got anywhere, his parental analyst would explain that waking up or feeling fear was a mistake. Everything that happened in a dream happened with a purpose, even though it might be beyond one's understanding while asleep. Falling was the fastest way to make contact with the powers of the spirit world, so falling itself was actually travelling toward the source of the spirit power that caused the fall. The child would then be reassured that the "falling spirits" loved him and were trying to call him to their land. If he relaxed, let go of his fear, and stayed asleep, he would be able to meet them.

The child might also be advised that if he became frightened of the enormous power of the falling spirits, he was still to persevere. Even if he found himself dying in a dream, this only meant he was receiving the spiritual power of the other world, something that was in any case his own spiritual power turned against him.

Although the terminology differs from that of Western psychology, the sophistication of such an analysis is extraordinary. Dr. Stewart noted that over a period of time, this mixture of social interaction, praise, and advice changed the fear of falling to a joy of flying. What began as an indwelling anxiety was transformed into an indwelling pleasure.

In his published report, Dr. Stewart offered several insights into the success of such a technique. It allowed children to realize they were still socially acceptable, even after revealing their deepest fears. It permitted them to take personal responsibility for their feelings. It released energy locked up in dream images. It showed how anxiety can block creativity. Most importantly, it diverted aggressive instincts into socially constructive channels—the reason why Senoi society had managed to avoid crimes of violence and intertribal aggression for so long.

The entire Senoi dream system, as outlined by Kilton Stewart, can be summarized as follows:

1. In dreams you must always confront and try to conquer danger. If the danger seems overwhelming, call on your friends

for help, but fight alone until they turn up. No real friend will harm you or refuse help in a dream. If you are attacked by someone who looks like a friend, recognize that this is not actually your friend but a spirit using his or her form as a mask to confuse you. (But make an effort in waking life to renew your friendship so the spirit cannot damage the relationship.) Thus you should always move toward danger and fight if necessary. Recognize that the power of your enemies is your power that they have stolen, so the more powerful your enemy, the more powerful you are. Once you attack and kill a dream enemy, the spirit of this enemy will always emerge as a servant or ally. Dream enemies are only frightening so long as you fail to come to grips with them.

2. Advance toward pleasure and continue with the pleasurable experience until you reach a resolution that will leave you with something of beauty or use in your society. Should you find yourself enjoying the experience of flying, for example, continue with your flight until you reach your destination, then meet the people or beings there and note their poetry, music, designs, or inventions, all or any of which may prove of benefit to you and/or your colleagues in waking life. If the pleasure is sexual, move through to orgasm, and having done so, ask your dream lover for a poem, song, dance, or something else that will express his or her beauty to your friends. (By doing this, you ensure no dream lover can steal the love that properly belongs to someone in your waking life.) Don't worry about incestuous or other forbidden liaisons as the dream lover is simply wearing a reassuring and familiar mask. You cannot overdo your sexual pleasure dreams since a rich love life in dreams indicates that the spirits of your emotional universe are favorably disposed to you.

3. Should you find yourself injuring, or even refusing to cooperate with, a friend or colleague during a dream, you should go

out of your way to express friendship and help to him or her on wakening. This is because the Senoi believe hostile spirits can only use the image of a friend for whom your store of goodwill is running low.

4. Achieve a positive result by converting negative experiences into their opposite. If you find yourself falling in your dream, try turning this into flying. Find out where the spirits want you to go. Explore the new environment and take careful note of it. Keep a careful lookout for anything of value in your waking life. Adapt this principle to all negative experiences you encounter.

Although these techniques intrigued a whole generation of Americans, Dr. Stewart's report attracted savage controversy. One critic claimed the Senoi didn't even have breakfast, let alone breakfast dream clinics. But whatever the truth about Dr. Stewart's claims, there is no doubt whatsoever that dreams may be used creatively.

Marie Jean Antoine Nicolas de Caritat, Marquis de Condorcet, the eighteenth-century French philosopher and advocate of educational reform, thought and wrote with much greater fluency and ease in his dreams than he did in waking life. The eighteenth-century Italian violinist Guiseppe Tartini first heard his *Devil's Sonata* in a dream and simply wrote it down upon waking. The English lyrical poet Samuel Taylor Coleridge did much the same with his famous work *Kubla Khan,* but was interrupted during the transcription process by a visitor and could not remember afterward how the dream poem ended. Saint Gennadius of Constantinople, the Byzantine theologian, became convinced of the immortality of his soul while conversing with an apparition in one of his dreams.

The nineteenth-century American engineer Elias Howe of Spencer, Massachusetts, solved the dilemma of making a sewing machine in a dream. In 1846, Howe was one of several inventors trying to crack the problem. He had little luck during his waking hours, but one night he dreamed he was captured by cannibals and put into a large cooking pot. As the cannibals danced around the fire, he noticed that their upraised spears had eye-holes in their tips and realized this was exactly what he needed to make his prototype sewing machine work properly. The great German chemist August Kekulé had a similar experience while working to discover the structure of the benzine molecule. He dreamed of a snake swallowing its own tail and saw at once that only a circular bonding of the molecule made any sense.

In 1940, as the Second World War got fully underway in Europe, the British electrical engineer D. B. Parkinson was involved in designing a carded potentiometer for telephones. Although his work was in the civilian arena with no apparent military application, he dreamed one night that he was on the European continent beside an Allied anti-aircraft gun. The weapon was proving extraordinarily successful: every time it was fired, it brought down a German plane. After several shots, one of the soldiers operating the gun called Parkinson over. As he drew closer, he discovered that the telephone control potentiometer he was working on had been mounted on the gun. The M9 gun director was a direct result of this dream. It was subsequently built and put to use with enormous success against German aircraft and buzzbombs.

These examples of dream creativity, which represent only the small tip of a large iceberg, occurred spontaneously, but many have claimed to be able to make creative use of their dreams quite purposely, exactly like the Senoi in Dr. Stewart's report. To do so, they have trained themselves in a technique inherent in Senoi dreamwork, but seldom mentioned in the literature. This is the technique of lucid dreaming.

LUCID DREAMS

In 1913, the Society for Psychical Research published in its *Proceedings* a paper by one of its members, the Dutch psychiatrist Frederik van Eeden, who had been making a study of his dreams since 1896.[1] In 352 out of 500 recorded dreams, van Eeden claimed he had full recollection of his waking life and could "act voluntarily" even though he was so fast asleep that no physical sensations penetrated his perceptions. He referred to experiences of this type as "lucid dreaming," the first time the term had ever been used.

"In these lucid dreams," van Eeden wrote, "the reintegration of the psychic functions is so complete that the sleeper remembers day-life and his own condition, reaches a state of perfect awareness, and is able to direct his attention, and to attempt different acts of free volition. Yet the sleep, as I am able confidently to state, is undisturbed, deep and refreshing."

---

1. Van Eeden, "A Study of Dreams."

The formal language may be a little confusing to modern readers, but when van Eeden begins to give examples, everything becomes perfectly clear. On the night of January 19–20, 1898, he dreamed he was lying on his stomach in his garden, watching his dog through the window of his study. Although this was his dream experience, he knew "with perfect certainty" that he *was* dreaming; he remembered that in reality, he was lying on his back in bed.

Van Eeden attempted an interesting experiment at this point. He resolved to wake up slowly, so he could observe how the (dream) sensation of lying on his stomach would change to the (waking) sensation of lying on his back. This he did and discovered that the transition was exactly like slipping from one body into another. He retained clear memories of his feelings both "in the garden" and in bed. Since the experience of double memory was repeated in many other lucid dreams, he concluded that it led "almost unavoidably" to the concept of a dream body.

"In a lucid dream," he wrote, "the sensation of having a body—having eyes, hands, a mouth that speaks, and so on—is perfectly distinct; yet I know at the same time that the physical body is sleeping and has quite a different position. In waking up the two sensations blend together, so to speak, and I remember as clearly the action of the dream-body as the restfulness of the physical body."

As more lucid dreams occurred, van Eeden continued to experiment. On one occasion he used saliva to draw a cross on his hand in order to find out whether the cross would still be there on his physical hand when he woke up. (It wasn't.) He also tried shouting in his dreams to see if his wife could hear him. (She couldn't.) On another occasion he tried to break a sheet of glass, but found it impervious. Later in the same dream, he took a delicate claret glass and tried to break that. It did break, but not until he had looked away, then looked back again some time later. He had the eerie impression of being in a fake world that very cleverly imitated the waking world, but with occasional failures.

Chapter 11

On several occasions van Eeden apparently awoke from lucid dreams only to discover he was still asleep and had only dreamed of waking. He also found it possible for a dream to slide in and out of lucidity, sometimes more than once. Lucid dreams enabled him to do many things that were simply impossible in the waking world, like flying or conversing with the dead.

Once, a lucid dream brought him an insight into the future that came true in waking life. In May of 1903, he had a dream encounter with his dead brother-in-law who told him financial disaster was close. At the time of the dream there was no indication at all of any problems with his finances, but shortly afterward a train of events began that was to ruin him. Curiously, the starting point had nothing to do with van Eeden himself—it was a national rail strike, the consequences of which could not have been logically predicted.

Van Eeden was not, of course, the first human being to have lucid dreams, he was merely the first Westerner to bring them to academic attention. At the time he did, the consensus belief, both within and without the scientific community, was that dreams were something that happened to you, a product, perhaps, of the unconscious mind but certainly beyond personal control. It is probably true to say most people believe this even today (as recently as January 6, 1990, the magazine *New Scientist* published an article by the British psychologist Susan Blackmore that dealt with lucid dreaming as if it were news), but outside the light of publicity, there has been extensive research into the lucid dream phenomenon that conclusively supports van Eeden's discovery that it is possible to become conscious while dreaming. Part of this research has shown the sensation of consciousness is no illusion. Lucid dreamers have been able to signal researchers using predetermined eye movements or changes in their breathing when they "woke up" within a dream.

But the most exciting discovery of all—noted, but not particularly emphasized by van Eeden—is that a lucid dream can be manipulated any way the dreamer wishes.[2] My wife, for example, was dreaming she was in a room of a friend's house when the dream went lucid and she realized she was dreaming. Since she knew lucid dreams could be controlled, it occurred to her that she would like some flowers. At once she found herself holding a bouquet of flowers. Delighted with this, she decided she would like more flowers. Instantly the entire room was filled with flowers.

Flowers are the least of the pleasures presented by lucid dreaming. The familiar laws of physics are suspended, so that you can do anything you wish and go anywhere you want. You can achieve your ideal weight and height at the blink of an eye. You can fly to Alpha Centauri without a spaceship. You can meet anyone you wish, become anything you wish, do anything you wish. You are limited only by the extent and creativity of your own imagination and since lucid dreams tend to be vivid dreams, the worlds you create can be so convincing they are extremely difficult to tell apart from the world of your waking hours. Indeed, studies carried out at Stanford University have shown that lucid dream experiences such as breathing, counting, singing, sexual activity, and the estimation of time all produce an effect on the physical brain—and sometimes even on the rest of the body— that appears identical to the effect of the waking experience.[3]

Since the dream/body influence goes far beyond the effect of waking imagery to produce real physiological effects, scientists have now begun to speculate about the possibility of using lucid dreams to facilitate therapeutic processes. They may also help personal development, enhanced self-confidence, and problem-solving. They have already been successfully used as a tool to combat recurring nightmares. There are particularly interesting

---

2. There is, however, one caveat: you have to believe you can do it. There have been instances in which lucid dreamers were unable to change their dreamscapes at will, but these seem to have been linked to lack of confidence.

3. LaBerge, *Lucid Dreaming*.

Chapter 11

applications for the handicapped who can, for all intents and purposes, regain full physical functionality during a lucid dream. Nor is this necessarily an empty illusion. One scientist has suggested that because of the body/mind interaction, sensorimotor practice of this type might help recovery from certain conditions, notably strokes.

The lifestyle benefits of lucid dreaming are also attracting considerable attention. The lucid dream has been compared to a flight simulator which allows pilots to train without the possibility of a fatal crash. Individuals might "try out" various courses of action in a lucid dream to experience their consequences before putting them into place in the waking world.

It is now clear that lucid dreams occur during periods of high-level activity in the autonomic nervous system. There is a decrease in pulse amplitude combined with increases both in the rate of breathing and eye-movement activity, even when compared to the movements that occur in normal REM sleep. During the first half-minute of lucidity, there is a decrease in alpha waves (which normally denote a state of relaxed alertness) at the back of the left brain hemisphere, indicating increased activation of the brain in that area. Since the left brain controls language, this activation may coincide with the dreamer mentally verbalizing the realization, "I am dreaming."

Many lucid dreams—perhaps as many as 80 percent of all reported cases—arise spontaneously when an ordinary dream turns lucid for no apparent reason. This is most likely to happen during nightmares or anxiety dreams, although there is evidence that any intense emotion, including embarrassment, anger, or joy, can trigger lucidity. Most people experience this type of lucid dream at least once in their lifetime but, exactly like an ordinary dream, may not remember it. Such lucid dreams tend to be short. I have kept a dream diary for more than a decade, during which I have had perhaps half a dozen or more. In each case, the realization of lucidity excited me so much I woke up almost at once.

Research shows most people do the same, but the experience can trigger a desire for more of the same. There are several techniques (and a few pieces of ingenious equipment) that can increase your chances. But before you can employ any of them, you need to train yourself to remember your dreams in the first place.

Despite the fact that everyone has multiple dreams each night, the average person recalls no more than one or two a week, and then only for a brief period. It is in the nature of the dreaming process that you will typically only remember your last dream of the night upon waking in the morning, but it will fade from your consciousness within seconds. Middle-of-the-night dreams will also be recalled if you happen to awaken from one, but again only for a few seconds.

Unfortunately, there is no easy road to dream recall. You need to leave a notebook and pen or a small tape recorder beside your bed and use them to record your dream immediately when you awaken. And that really *is* immediately; wait a few seconds and the dream will begin to fade. Even if you awaken several times throughout the night, you are unlikely to catch all your dreams, but this cannot be helped. Try for as many as you can manage.

In the early stages, you should force yourself to write down every detail of the dream you can remember. Dreams typically have their own structure that differs considerably from the familiar cause and effect of waking life. Don't try to make sense of your dream; simply record it as you experienced it with all its peculiarities intact.

Later, as recall improves, you can reduce your dream recording to notes of the salient points which you can expand on as you write up your dream journal. If you find you have no dream recall at all, there are a couple of tricks you can try. One is to return to the sleeping position you were in when you awoke. For some reason this tends to stimulate dream memories. Another is to try to capture the "feel" of your dream rather than details of the dream itself. You can usefully ask yourself questions like:

"Was the dream pleasant or unpleasant?"

"Did it take place in the city or in the country?"

"Did any of my friends appear?"

"Was there a particular theme?"

"What was the overall shape of my dream?"

First thing in the morning, transcribe your notes into a dream journal and date each entry. Work hard to make both the note-taking and the morning transcription a habit. The longer you leave making a definitive record of your dream, the more difficult it becomes. Even with notes, small details tend to disappear.

Dream recording is an antisocial occupation unless you sleep alone,[4] but the good news is that after a few months, you will find your dream recall improves to the point where you can dispense with the note-taking (although not with recording details in your journal). If you *do* sleep with a partner, it is a good idea to discuss your dreams when awake like the Senoi, as this will strongly underpin the recall. Some authorities suggest that the act of recording your dreams tends, in itself, to stimulate lucid dreaming. Whatever about this, it is a good idea to concentrate on simple dream recording, without worrying about lucidity, for two to three months before you start to apply lucidity techniques.

Perhaps the simplest of lucidity techniques is autosuggestion. This is not a particularly effective method (it works in only about 14 percent of cases; less than one in five), but it is so easy, it is certainly worth a try. Immediately before retiring, write down the affirmation, "I will have a lucid dream tonight," and sign it with

---

4. It's a good idea to equip yourself with a small flashlight so you can make notes in the night without switching on a light. There is even a special pen you can buy from the Lucidity Institute (www.lucidity.com) that shines just enough light to allow you to write.

your name as if it were a formal legal document. If you can have it witnessed, so much the better. Although the procedure sounds silly, it can sometimes have sufficient impact on your subconscious mind to do the trick.

Another interesting and extremely old method is to use a quartz crystal. In shamanic lore, quartz is one of the few substances that has an astral (inner, imaginal) structure that precisely matches its physical appearance.[5] Because of this, quartz makes an excellent doorway to the inner levels—one reason, perhaps, for its popularity in shamanic practice worldwide. Select a clear quartz point and cleanse it using spring water with a little added salt. Spend time examining the crystal until you are completely familiar with its appearance, including any interior flaws or features. Next, ask your crystal to help you in your efforts to trigger lucid dreams. If this makes you feel even sillier than the signed affirmation described above, you can console yourself with the knowledge that here again you are simply trying to influence your unconscious mind.

With these preliminaries complete, leave your crystal on your bedside table and as you go to bed, make a pact with yourself to look for the crystal in your dreams. Like the written affirmation, this does not work for everyone, but for those it does, finding the crystal tends to trigger lucidity.

Many of the remaining techniques require a greater or lesser degree of self-training; and it is probably true to say that the more effort you put into this, the greater your chances of beginning to dream lucidly. The following, in ascending order of effort, are the most popular methods.

---

5. To understand what this means, it may be useful for you to recall times when you have met up with friends in dreams. In many instances, they look nothing like the way they look in waking life, yet, in the dream, you somehow know the friends' identities without difficulty. In these cases, the inner, astral appearance of the friend does not match the physical.

RECOGNITION OF ANOMALIES

This method is based on the common observation that waking life tends to follow strict rational rules, while dreams do not. Instead of attempting to go lucid directly as you did with the previous two techniques, you should bend your attention toward looking for anomalies, both in your environment and in your behavior. If, for example, you suddenly find yourself surrounded by purple leprechauns dancing a hornpipe, the chances are extremely high that you are dreaming. By recognizing the anomaly, you simultaneously realize you are dreaming and lucidity occurs.

Recognizing anomalies in your own behavior requires a real degree of self-observation in your waking state. But once you have gained the self-knowledge, you will be speedily aware of any unusual reactions in dreams. You might, perhaps, find yourself shrieking angrily at someone when your innate good manners would normally prevent such a display. Or you could find yourself making love to someone other than your spouse. These things are not absolute indicators of a dream—unusual behavior is obviously not completely unknown in waking life—but they should be enough to arouse suspicion, which is usually all that is needed to trigger lucidity if you really are dreaming.

Lucidity cues of this type, known as "dreamsigns" by researchers, can be extremely subtle. One sleeper only discovered he was dreaming by measuring the length of his shadow. He had calculated from the position of the sun that it should have been equal to his height. When he discovered it was shorter, he concluded, with considerable reluctance since the experience was so vivid, that he was dreaming.

PROGRAMMED BEHAVIOR

This method, which is really a variation on the anomaly technique given above, is based on training yourself to take certain actions that tend to produce quite different results in dreams than they do in waking life. Attempting to fly (without an airplane) is an obvious example. If you flap your arms in waking life, you will usually only succeed in looking like a chicken. The same action in a dream may well result in lift-off. In essence, what you are attempting here is to *create* the anomalies that result in lucidity.

Developing the habit of rereading text may prove very useful. It is a curious fact that text that appears in a dream has a distinct tendency to differ if you go back and read it a second time. Once you realize this, changing text becomes a lucidity cue.

Rather like using the crystal, you can decide to make virtually any type of action or encounter into a cue. The author Carlos Castaneda suggested looking at your hands, an action used in several esoteric practices. In dreams, this sometimes results in an anomaly—if you are caucasian, they may appear black, or vice versa—but even without changes, the hand examination acts as a reminder to ask yourself if you are dreaming. You are, in essence, setting a memory trigger.

REPEATED DREAMS

This method does not confine itself to recurring dreams, although recurring dreams certainly fall into the category. The trick here is to cultivate a growing awareness of your dreams. You can do this by reading through your dream journal at frequent intervals, looking for recurring themes or locations. Once you do this, you will find that as you dream, you will sometimes realize you have had a similar dream before. This realization tends to act as a lucidity trigger.

M.I.L.D

One of the world's leading authorities on lucid dreaming, Dr. Stephen LaBerge of Stanford University, developed mnemonic induction of lucid dreams (M.I.L.D.) for his doctrinal thesis and used it with such success that he can now dream lucidly at will. Thankfully, the method is now generally referred to by its acronym M.I.L.D.

This technique is specifically applied after you wake from a dream and before you go back to sleep again. The first step is to focus on the dream and try to remember it in as much detail as possible. Then, as you begin to drift back toward sleep, focus clearly on your intention that when you begin to dream again, you will realize you are dreaming. You should begin a mental mantra: "Next time I dream, I will remember that I'm dreaming." Try to focus on this single idea. As in meditation practice, if you find your mind drifting on to other things, gently bring it back again to the mantra.

With your mind firmly focused on the intent of remembering, imagine yourself back in the dream from which you have just awakened. But this time imagine yourself realizing you are dreaming. (You might do this by applying the dreamsign method outlined above. Once you find the element that proves you are in a dream, imagine telling yourself firmly that you are dreaming.) Carry on with your visualization by imagining, in detail, how you would have changed the dream had you become lucid, then imagine yourself doing so in the lucid dream you are about to have when you fall asleep. Repeat your mantra and visualization until you do so.

NAPPING

If you wake during sleep, then fall asleep again, your chances of a lucid dream increase naturally. This means that napping—short, generally light periods of sleep—can become an excellent route to lucidity when handled properly.

Set your alarm so you wake up an hour earlier than usual in the morning. Stay awake for approximately thirty minutes, during which you should think or read about lucid dreaming, then return to sleep while practicing the M.I.L.D. technique. This simple change of routine increases your chances of success some fifteen to twenty times.

REALITY TESTS

Reality testing is one of the more disturbing methods of inducing lucid dreams, but like M.I.L.D., it is one of the most successful. Set yourself to perform a reality test several times each day. You can, and should, do these any time the thought occurs to you, but it can be extremely useful to set specific times. You might, for example, test each time you arrive at work, get into your car, see yourself in a mirror, eat a meal, or look at your watch. Although reality testing feels odd, the more often you do it, the more effective the method becomes.

The reality test itself breaks down into three stages. For the first, you need to equip yourself with a written text or a digital watch. When the time comes to carry out your test, read the text or look at the numbers on your watch. Then look away and look back to see if they change. (You might even try to *make* them change.) If you are dreaming, the text will change three-quarters of the time on a first rereading and almost 100 percent of the time on a second rereading. So a change in text, or even a text that looks odd or has ceased to make sense, indicates you are dreaming. If the text is stable after several rereadings, there is an excellent chance you are awake (although it is not a certainty; you can get a stable text in a dream about 5 percent of the time).

Assuming you *are* awake, you should then, for the second stage of your test, imagine that your surroundings are actually a dream. Imagine that things shift and change the way they do in a dream. You are not trying to persuade yourself that you actually are dreaming, but simply attempting to imagine what it might be like *if* you were. But make your visualization as vivid as possible. Once you have caught the feeling you are dreaming, move on to the next stage.

The final stage of your reality check is to visualize yourself greatly enjoying a particular dream activity. You might like to imagine something you plan to do during your next lucid dream—an experiment in levitation, a sexual encounter, or whatever—and visualize yourself enjoying doing so now. Once the reality check sequence becomes a habitual part of your behavior, it will eventually begin to intrude into your dreams with the inevitable result of lucidity.

W.I.L.D.

W.I.L.D. is another acronym beloved by lucid dreamers. It stands for "wake induced lucid dreaming" and is one of the more difficult techniques to apply. Essentially it involves passing directly from the waking state into the dream state *without losing consciousness.*

Although this must seem an obvious impossibility to most of us, the process is described in Tibetan literature and confirmed by modern Western research. The method is easily enough explained, but requires considerable practice. Your best time to attempt a W.I.L.D. is immediately after waking in the morning or during a period of naps. Focus on your last dream and relax as you try mentally to "reach" for it. Maintain concentration; if you allow your mind to drift, the chances are you will fall asleep. You are very likely to experience both visual and auditory hypnagogic imagery before passing into the dream state proper. After this you may well feel yourself sinking or floating out of your body, an experience similar to that of astral projection. Alternatively, you could find yourself "drawn" into the dream; one subject reported being grabbed by a wind. Even the most experienced practitioner may have a momentary loss of consciousness, but this should be extremely brief if it occurs at all. When the transition is completed, you will be dreaming and lucid.

America's Lucidity Institute, accessible on the Internet at www.lucidity.com, offers some interesting technology designed to aid the development of lucid dreaming. Devices like the NovaDreamer and DreamLight incorporate sleep masks with built-in sensors that detect the rapid eye movements that indicate a dream period has begun. The gadgets then send a signal—which may be a flashing light or an audible cue—to alert the user he or she is dreaming. No one claims such devices, which can involve quite a substantial financial investment, will guarantee lucid dreams, but they can work to support the various self-training methods outlined above and may for some people speed up the process.

But achieving a lucid dream state may not be enough. One very common difficulty is maintaining it. Your dream goes lucid, but before you can do much with it, you wake up. Alternatively, your dream goes lucid but after a time you lose the lucidity. Fortunately techniques have evolved to deal with both of these problems.

Often the signal that you are about to awaken is a fading of the dream. But if you examine your situation carefully, you will usually find it is only the visual element that is fading, especially at first. When this happens, you can often stabilize the dream by locking your attention on one of the remaining elements. You might, for example, try listening to voices, beginning a conversation, or reaching out to feel dream objects. You could also concentrate on any smells or tastes present in the dream.

Your dream body and the dream ground beneath your feet are two of the most persistent elements of any dream and consequently tend to be the last to fade. Because of this, looking at the ground or your own hands or feet will tend to prevent your wakening. So will opening and closing your dream eyes, rubbing your dream face, or carrying out virtually any action that focuses your attention on your body.

Other useful techniques are consciously relaxing the dream body, purposely falling and spinning. All three of these methods will sometimes lead you to believe you have actually awoken, but the routine tests will quickly show you have only dreamed of waking and lucidity will return. Of the three, the most effective seems to be spinning. The first sign of waking is usually a loss of color in your surroundings, followed fairly quickly by the disappearance of visual detail. You find yourself in a faded, washed-out world in which the light begins to dim. As soon as you become aware of any of these signs, extend your arms and spin like a dervish. Concentrate on the sensation of spinning and remind yourself that anything you see, hear, or feel will probably be a dream. Although this technique will sometimes revive the old dream, more often than not it will generate a new dream environment (including the illusion of having wakened) so dreamsign checks are usually in order. (If, incidentally, you do wake up despite everything, you might try staying absolutely motionless and relaxing your body deeply. There is a good chance you will slip straight back into the dream state.)

Loss of lucidity tends to be a beginner's problem, although it can happen even to experts from time to time. If it *does* happen, the habitual application of the methods that generated lucidity in the first place will almost always cause it to return. But if you find yourself frequently losing lucidity, an excellent preventative is to talk to yourself in the dream. Specifically, you should continually remind yourself that you are dreaming—let "This is all a dream" become your mantra. It is also an excellent idea to watch out for dream situations or experiences that tend to make you lose lucidity. Once you learn to recognize them, you can usually retain lucidity by a simple act of will.

Having mastered the art of lucid dreaming, you are faced with the problem of what to do with it. Several worthy possibilities were mentioned earlier—personal development, therapy, and so on—but research has shown that most lucid dreamers in the West use their newfound talent to facilitate interesting sexual encounters, especially in the early stages of their experiments.

Tibetan masters have, however, gone a very different route. In doing so, they have developed several lucid dream techniques of their own, and gone beyond lucid dreaming altogether.

12

DREAM YOGA

According to the ancient doctrines of Tibet, no dream is random. The mechanism of dreaming, which determines dream content, is related to the subtle rlung (pranic energies) within the body.

Tibetans believe that your mind and energy system work in tandem. Prana is often described as a blind horse that has the potential to move about easily but does not know where it is going. Mind, on the other hand, is seen as a lame rider—it can see where it might go, but is unable to travel to or, more importantly, remain in a particular place without great difficulty. The two together form a unit that functions a great deal more effectively than either would alone, but only when the rider learns to control the horse. When an untrained rider and horse get together, they often gallop far and wide, but usually without very much control over where they are going.

As you lose awareness of the physical world in the process of falling asleep, your mind is carried by the blind horse of rlung energy into a specific chakra. For the unenlightened, the goal chakra is absolutely determined by the karmic traces fixed within the energy itself. Each chakra is believed to be a doorway into one of the six realms we studied earlier (Hell, Hungry Ghost, Animal, Human, Demi-God, and God), which is another way of saying that each chakra is associated with a particular level of consciousness.

The trigger that leads the mind to be drawn into a chakra is often something that happened to you during the day. You might, for example, have exchanged angry words with your spouse or suffered a bitter disappointment in love. The incident then activates an established karmic trace associated with the heart chakra. Thus, in sleep, your mind is drawn into that same chakra and the experience manifests as a dream.

Potentially, each dream provides an opportunity to deal with some aspect of your accumulated karma. Since Tibetans believe dreams and waking consciousness are simply twin poles of the human mind, your reactions in a dream are just as capable of discharging karma, or laying down fresh karmic traces, as your reactions in waking life. Unfortunately, most of us remain ignorant of the spiritual possibilities presented by dreams, and incapable of taking advantage of them even should they be pointed out. For this reason, Tibetan dream yoga was developed. Among its aims is the centering of mind and rlung energy in the body's midline channel. If this can be achieved, dreaming becomes (relatively) free of personal karmic influences (although not, as we shall see, free of collective karma), which permits the emergence of two new types of dreams. Tibetans call them dreams of clarity and clear light dreams.

Dreams of clarity are essentially knowledge dreams. As you become increasingly proficient in dream yoga, your dreams become clearer, more vivid, and detailed. Such dreams are not (necessarily) lucid, but they tend to be more easily remembered and do represent an increased awareness of the dream state. You will already know how, in ordinary dreams, you can be swept from one scene to another, one experience to another, with little rhyme or reason. Everything is fluid and shifting, near impossible to follow in any rational way. Dreams of clarity are far more stable and you are far more stable within them. This reflects the fact that the blind horse and lame rider have ceased to be buffeted by personal karmic winds, but have emerged from the chakras to take refuge in the central channel.

In dreams of clarity, you are still presented with images and experiences, but the information embodied in them is no longer the result of your personal karma. It is drawn instead from a transpersonal source. Such dreams may offer teachings from divine beings or dream representations of your guru and as such may become a useful guide to your spiritual practice. Dreams of clarity do not, however, embody the ultimate experience of illumination since collective karma, largely generated by your cultural environment, remains in operation and maintains the illusion of duality.

Although a dream of clarity can arise for anyone, the experience is rare until you become proficient in dream yoga. Tibetan masters warn that not all dreams that present the appearance of spiritual guidance are necessarily dreams of clarity. If you have an interest in esoteric matters (and have perhaps just begun some form of spiritual practice), it is very natural that you might dream of such things. But dreams of this sort, which arise before mind and rlung energies become stable, are almost always driven by karma, and the doctrines they present shift and change with the activation of each new karmic trace.

You may have encountered people who have become victims of karmic "knowledge" dreams. They seem to be incapable of making the simplest decision without some form of "spirit guidance." Keeping up with orders from their "inner contacts" becomes a full-time occupation. They become locked in a personal drama of their own manufacture and see signs and portents everywhere. Their only real hope is to develop discrimination and learn to separate out the rare dreams that contain genuine spiritual wisdom from the many that arise from personal fantasies.

Clear light dreams can take a decade or more of yoga practice to emerge since they arise out of the pristine rlung energy in the central channel untainted by any karmic trace. They are of two types. One can scarcely be called a dream at all since it involves a nondual state of voidness free from images or even thought. The other is more difficult to describe since mental activities, including dream images, continue to manifest but the individual has ceased to experience them in dualist terms. Because ego has vanished, thoughts and images are no longer seen as somehow "out there" with the individual as an observer. Rather everything that which is experienced and the individual experiencing it becomes a seamless whole.

If you are familiar with Asian doctrines, you may have noted the similarities between the clear light dream state and states of mystical enlightenment or even nirvana. This is by no means accidental. Tibetans refer to the experience of nonduality as *rigpa*, an enlightened state in which the individual at long last realizes there is no boundary between him and the whole of manifest existence; all is everything, all is unity, and the only ultimate reality is that of the clear light void. Various yogas are designed to spark such a realization, leaving their practitioners in increasingly long periods of rigpa. But since dreaming and waking consciousness are simply two aspects of the same mind, the development of the rigpa state during the day leads inevitably to "clear light" (rigpa) dreaming at night. Conversely, the practice of dream yoga which leads to a "clear light" dream will tend to stimulate the experience of rigpa during the daytime.

The whole of Tibetan dream yoga is driven by a realization that karmic traces tend to lock us into a state of ignorance. In order to break the lock, we need to become constantly aware of how we generate, and regenerate, karmic traces. This awareness enables us to break the habits of several lifetimes and cultivate nonattachment. Clearly, the more time you devote to your efforts, the sooner you will get results. Tibetans, a superlatively pragmatic people, long ago decided that since we spend approximately a third of our lives asleep, it made good sense to develop a "Practice of the Night." It gives you more time to engage in spiritual disciplines and does not interfere with the practicalities of daily life. (Although the ultimate goal might be a nirvana in which all opposites are reconciled, we have to live in a dualistic world until we get there. So things like earning a living are important.)

But in order to practice spiritual disciplines while you are asleep, you need to be aware of your current state, otherwise there is no possibility of control over what you do. The most advanced yogic masters actually manage to retain conscious awareness throughout the entire sleep state, something that is almost incomprehensible to Western science. The rest settle for conscious awareness during dreams; in other words, lucid dreaming.

The Tibetan system for achieving (then going beyond) lucidity differs from the various Western techniques we have already examined. It embodies the familiar platforms of Tibetan occultism: sonics, visualization, mind control, and manipulation of the rlung energies. Since the successful dream yogi must have sufficient control to avoid being swept away in the tidal wave of karmic traces that typically manifest in dreams, the practice begins not with dreamwork at all, but with a particular meditation designed to stabilize the mind. The meditation is known as "Calm Abiding," *zhiné* in Tibetan, and is virtually identical to the Western religious practice of contemplation. The technique begins with the mind fixed on a single object and develops over time to a stage when the mind can be held fixed without the necessity for an objective focus. The three stages of the practice are known as Forceful Zhiné, Natural Zhiné, and Ultimate Zhiné.

Although Calm Abiding can use any object when practiced for its own sake, as a preparation for dream yoga, Tibetan gurus often suggest the use of the Tibetan letter *A* which looks like this:

Make up a meditation card. Although the card itself may be square, it should contain five concentric circles. The innermost, just over an inch in diameter, is to be indigo, the next blue, the next green, then red, yellow, and white. In the center circle, carefully paint the Tibetan letter *A* so it emerges white out of the indigo background. Now fix the card to a rod long enough to place it at eye level when you are seated cross-legged. Attach the rod to a base.

To begin your practice, you are required to be seated in a comfortable cross-legged posture with your hands folded in your lap, palms upward, one on top of the other. Hold your spine straight but not rigid, and tuck your chin in to straighten your neck. Set your card-stand in front of you about eighteen inches away from your eyes. If you have made it correctly, you should be able to look at the card without raising or lowering your eyes. Let your eyes relax; they should be neither wide open nor shut. Breathe normally and fix your gaze on the object. Remain quite still and try to focus your concentration exclusively on the white Tibetan *A*.

You will find this extremely difficult at first, especially if you have limited experience of meditation. Your mind will tend to slide away to think of other things. You will be distracted by any movement or noise around you. But each time you experience a distraction, bring your mind back to the card. After a few moments, you will quickly realize why this is called the stage of Forceful Zhiné. The practice is only possible if you keep forcing your mind back time and again to the object of your contemplation. In the early stages, it can be quite helpful to take frequent breaks rather than attempting one long meditative session, but even during breaks try to remember that this is purely a short, temporary rest from a difficult spiritual practice.

What you are attempting is the exact mental equivalent of exercising a muscle. You have to keep at it if you want results. Push against your limits and, with time, the mental muscle will grow progressively stronger.

As you gaze at the object of your contemplation, try not to think about it. If you find yourself engaged in an inner dialogue such as, "This is the letter *A* in Tibetan . . . it's an interesting shape," and so on, then you are falling short of your goal. What you want is a simple, present-moment *awareness* of the letter; no more and no less. Allow your breathing to calm until you are no longer aware of it. Allow your body to relax. Allow your mind to sink deeper and deeper into a state of calm and peace, but guard against falling asleep or into trance.

At this stage, and perhaps even at later stages, you may find yourself subject to unusual physical sensations. These are a natural outcome of what you are trying to do—the mind resists training and will distract you if it can!—and can be ignored.

With practice, things will become easier and easier. You will find the periods of time free of mind-wandering become progressively longer until, suddenly, you will be able to contemplate the symbol on the card without having to force your attention back again and again. You have entered the stage of Natural Zhiné.

At this point you can embark on a very interesting experiment. Try to achieve the same mental state without the symbol. Put away the card and see if you can focus your attention on empty space. An expanse of clear sky is probably best as something to look at, but any area of space will do. Remember, you are not trying to focus on a point within this space, but on the space itself. Stay calm and relaxed and allow your mind to diffuse throughout the whole of the space you are contemplating. Tibetans call this "dissolving the mind," a wonderfully expressive description of the experience.

When you dissolve the mind successfully, you enter the third stage of the exercise, Ultimate Zhiné. You may or may not recognize your achievement. (If you were a student in Tibet, your guru would alert you.) It is not characterized by any dramatic transition, but rather by a certain ease and lightness. You will find that your thoughts arise and then dissolve without effort or influence. Look carefully—this is something else your guru would have pointed out to you—and you will be able to differentiate between the *functioning* of your mind, in the form of thoughts or pictures, and the steady, unvarying *presence* of the mind itself.

Properly directed, Zhiné practice alone can take you a long way on the mystic path, but for many practitioners, it is the initial step toward the fascinating experiences of dream yoga. The first practice of dream yoga itself involves an attempt to reduce the chaos of the typical dream state by making some changes in your karmic traces. The method used to do this is similar to the Western lucid dream practice of reality testing, but with one very important difference.

In the West, prospective lucid dreamers embark on a (waking) regimen that involves their stopping from time to time to make sure they are truly awake. As reality testing becomes habitual, the theory is that they will begin to carry out the same instinctive tests while asleep. Once they do, it is easy to determine they are actually dreaming and the dream itself goes lucid.

Westerners engaged in this practice take it for granted there is an essential difference between the waking state and the dream. When awake, you function in the real world; dreaming you don't. The distinction is not nearly so clear-cut for Tibetans. Thus the "reality check" of the West, designed to differentiate between waking reality and dreaming illusion, is replaced by an "unreality check" designed to remind that asleep or awake, *everything* you experience is an illusion. Tibetan dream gurus advise that throughout your waking day, you continually remind yourself you are living in a dream. The car you drive is a dream car. The building where you work is a dream building. The money you make is dream money. All appearances are creations of your mind.

It is not enough simply to keep repeating, "This is all a dream." You need to make the effort to feel it in your bones, to realize the profound truth you are expressing. Use your imagination and anything else that helps. Oddly enough, this practice does not turn your waking world into a shimmering heat mirage, but rather makes it more vivid and gives you a greater sense of presence, signs that indicate you are properly engaged with your spiritual work and have not sunk into habitual repetition.

The focus of the technique needs to be as much on yourself as your environment. After all, if everything is a dream, then you are the dreamer. But that means you are dreaming the body with indigestion and arthritis, the anger at your boss, and the disappointment with your children. You are also, let it be said, dreaming the lust that possesses you, the pleasure of friendship, the happiness you sometimes feel when facing a new dawn. All these things, which you have believed for a lifetime to be your very essence, are no more than the creations of your mind.

As you engage in the practice, a change occurs in your outlook. You begin to realize that everything happening is both transient and intimately related to the projections of your mind. This inevitably changes your reaction to events, something which, in the past, has been largely unconscious anyway. Life has less power over you since you are no longer handing your own power over to it. You may recall the Tibetan belief that karmic traces are generated by reactions rather than experiences or even actions. Against this background, it follows that in changing your reactions by coming to recognize the illusory quality of life, you will tend to generate fewer karmic traces. The karmic change leads in turn to a change in dream content.

(Although not part of Tibetan dream yoga theory, it is easy to see how the habitual questioning of the reality of your waking state must sooner or later lead to your questioning the nature of your dream state. Once the pertinent question is asked, lucidity follows.)

A consequence of the "unreality check"—seen by Tibetans as a separate stage of the practice—is a decrease in both desire and aversion. Letting go in this way is a powerful antidote to depression, anger, envy, and other unhappy states.

The next stage of dream yoga involves a variation on a technique that will be familiar to many Western occultists: the evening review. The evening review is itself a very simple exercise. You are required to go over the events of the day immediately before you fall asleep, simply recalling each one without passion or judgment. In the Tibetan variation, you are urged to view your recollections as memories of dreams. Use your intellect to comprehend this fully—any memory shares many characteristics with a dream, after all—and try to see the projections that sustained your experiences. It is very useful to note the differences that arise when you relate to an experience as a dream and when you relate to it as something real and solid.

When you complete your review, focus your intent on recognizing the events of the night for the dreams they are. Tibetan gurus see this as "sending a wish" and this viewpoint, too, can be useful. Try to experience your intent as a prayer to your inner teachers or gods, promising to do your best to recognize the true nature of your dreams and asking their help in the endeavor.

In the morning, you should make an effort to remember the dreams of the night. This may not be easy at first and it is perfectly permissible to leave a notebook or tape recorder beside your bed so you can make notes. As you recall your dreams, see them for the illusions they were and determine to recognize the illusory quality of your experiences in the coming day.

Taken together, these techniques follow a twenty-four-hour wheel of spiritual practice aimed at convincing you that both your inner and your outer worlds have the essence of *maya*.

THE PRACTICE
OF THE NIGHT

Tibetan mystics take sleep seriously. They believe that purifying the mind before retiring for the night generates greater presence in dreams, reduces karmic influences, and ensures a more positive experience altogether. A purified mind is particularly important should you embark on the path of dream yoga. One way of achieving it is known as the Nine Purifications Breathing.

NINE PURIFICATIONS BREATHING

This exercise is based on the observation that stress influences the way you breathe. Tibetans long ago decided to find out whether the reverse was true—that the way you breathe might influence your stress levels. They discovered that it does and developed the Nine Purifications Breathing as a result.

Begin by sitting cross-legged in your usual meditation position: spine straight but not rigid, chin tucked in to straighten your neck, and hands placed palms up in your lap, left hand on top of your right.

Now visualize the three major channels of energy within your body, the rtsa discussed in chapter 4. For this exercise there is no need to visualize the chakras; concentrate instead on picturing the channels clearly. Establish the central channel first. It is roughly three-eighths inch in diameter and runs through the center of your body, widening a little from the level of your heart to the crown of your head. It is a clear blue in color.

When you can see the central channel clearly in your mind's eye, turn your attention to the two side channels. These are narrower than the central channel, about the diameter of a pencil. These channels curve round to join with the center channel at the base of your body, some four inches below your navel. They rise parallel to the center channel on either side, curve up over the skull, and down behind the eyes to form a complete circuit. Some authorities note they have openings as the nostrils, indicating the close relationship between the breath and the body's subtle energies.

Like the central channel, each of the side channels has a distinctive color, but this differs depending on your sex. If you are male, the channel in the right hand side of your body is white while that in the left side is red. If you are female, the colorings are reversed—your right channel is red and the left white. This difference in channel coloring is reflected in slight variations in the Nine Purifications technique which also depend on whether you are a man or a woman.

Although most practices, including this one, concentrate on the three major energy channels, there are, in fact, a great many other energy flows throughout your body. The various yoga postures and hand gestures, called *mudras,* are designed to influence these flows in subtle ways. A simple mudra involved in the Nine Purifications is simply pressing your thumb against the base of your ring finger.

To begin the exercise proper, follow this sequence:

Men

1. Press your right thumb against the base of your right ring finger. Raise your right hand and close off your right nostril with the ring finger. Inhale green light through your left nostril. Now close off your left nostril (again using your right ring finger) and exhale completely through the right nostril. As you exhale, imagine yourself expelling all masculine problems and obstacles from the white channel. As you do so, the air you exhale should be visualized as turning light blue. This represents one Purification. Repeat the process until you have completed three rounds of inhalation and exhalation.

2. Change hands and complete another three rounds of inhalation and exhalation exactly as before, but using the opposite nostril. Each time you exhale, imagine you are expelling all feminine problems and obstacles from the red channel. As you do so, the air you exhale should be visualized as turning pale pink. This completes six of the Nine Purifications.

3. Ensure your left hand is on top of your right, palm upward in your lap. Inhale green light into both nostrils. Imagine it as a healing balm moving down the two side channels until it reaches the junction with the center channel at the base. On your out-breath, visualize the light moving up the center channel to emerge from the top of your head. As you do so, imagine all problems and illnesses associated with malevolent spirits expelled from the top of your head in the form of black smoke. Three rounds of this practice complete the Nine Purifications.

Women

1. Press your left thumb against the base of your left ring finger. Raise your left hand and close off your left nostril with the ring finger. Inhale green light through your right nostril. Now close off your right nostril (again using your left ring finger)

and exhale completely through the left nostril. As you exhale, imagine yourself expelling all masculine problems and obstacles from the white channel. As you do so, the air you exhale should be visualized as turning light blue. This represents one Purification. Repeat the process until you have completed three rounds of inhalation and exhalation.

2. Change hands and complete another three rounds of inhalation and exhalation exactly as before, but using the opposite nostril. Each time you exhale, imagine you are expelling all feminine problems and obstacles from the red channel. As you do so, the air you exhale should be visualized as turning pale pink. This completes six of the Nine Purifications.

3. Ensure your left hand is on top of your right, palm upward in your lap. Inhale green light into both nostrils. Imagine it as a healing balm moving down the two side channels until it reaches the junction with the center channel at the base. On your out-breath, visualize the light moving up the center channel to emerge from the top of your head. As you do so, imagine all problems and illnesses associated with malevolent spirits expelled from the top of your head in the form of black smoke. Three rounds of this practice complete the Nine Purifications.

After the Nine Purifications, you can get into bed and begin the exercises designed to get your dreams in order and, eventually, trigger lucidity. Perhaps the simplest of the exercises is the following.

Take a few deep breaths to calm and steady yourself, then focus your concentration on visualizing a white representation of the letter *A* in the center of your body. Since the letter must be associated with its relevant sound—"ahhh"—you may prefer to use the English letter *A* although this obviously does not figure in the original Tibetan texts. Like many esoteric practices, this variation can be approached in the spirit of trial and error: if it works for you, use it. Purists, however, will prefer the original Tibetan symbol which, fortunately, you will already have learned to visualize clearly if you carried out the zhiné meditations given in chapter 12:

Whether an English *A* or Tibetan ཨ་, bear in mind that both symbols represent the same "ahhh" sound. Hear that sound in your mind as if it were uttered from the symbol itself.

Try to focus your mind on the symbol for as long as possible, but if this proves difficult, it is worth realizing that the important point is to have the symbol mentally in place *as you fall asleep.* Should you find yourself having difficulties with a static visualization, try imagining that a second symbol emerges from the first, then a third from the second until a chain of them reaches from your heart area all the way up to the crown of your head. Now, symbol by symbol, see the chain retreat back down until there is a single central symbol once more. Repeat this process until you fall asleep. Although it sounds difficult, it actually has a soporific effect, rather like the famous "counting sheep."

The real trick, however, is to practice until the whole process becomes instinctive. When you reach that stage, you no longer feel you are visualizing the imaginal symbol, but rather calling it up. Once this is achieved, the symbol will persist with no effort on your part. Consequently you can relax completely and allow yourself to move into the sleep state with both your concentration and the symbol itself intact. Correctly performed, the exercise leads to lucidity, although this is seen as a secondary effect. The main goal is to balance the energies in the central channel and consequently, you are advised to re-establish the symbol and sound the "ahhh" immediately upon wakening.

A more complex practice with essentially the same goal begins by advising you to lie in a particular way as you prepare for sleep. Men should lie on their right side, women on their left, and both with their head in the north. Draw up your knees a little to give stability to the position, rest your head in the palm of your underneath hand, and leave your upper arm straight along your body. Relax and calm your breathing until it is no longer audible.

Visualize a red, four-petalled lotus at the position of your throat chakra. Mentally place a luminous Tibetan *A* (ཨ་) at its center and note how the symbol picks up the color of the petals. Visualize the Tibetan syllables "ra," "sha," "la," and "sa" respectively at the front, back, left, and right of each petal. The appearance of these syllables is:

"ra"   "sha"   "la"   "sa"

Keep your mind focused on the central ཨ་ (*A*) as you fall asleep. Sleep for two hours (set the alarm clock if necessary) then move on to the next part of the practice. Get back into your initial sleeping position, if you are not still in it, then inhale and gently hold your breath. Clench the muscles of your pelvic floor so there is a sensation of pushing the breath upward to compress it just below the navel. Hold your breath for a few seconds longer, then release it while simultaneously relaxing all the muscles of your body, including those of the chest and pelvic floor.

As you engage in the breathing exercise, bring your attention to your "third eye," the brow chakra located just above the point where your eyebrows meet. Visualize a small luminous ball of white light there. Try to feel the ball as if it was physically there.

At first, your efforts will be expended simply on the visualization, but as happened with previous visualizations, there will come a time when this one becomes automatic and requires no effort to hold. When this happens, you can begin to allow your mind to merge with the light from this little sphere to become increasingly clear. You will find this stage of the exercise not only stimulates lucid dreams, but can actually help you maintain a continuity of consciousness between waking and sleeping states.

The next part of the practice comes two hours after the last.[1] Once more you should awaken (with the alarm clock if necessary), but this time you need to adopt a new sleeping position. Stack your pillows high and lie on your back with your legs loosely crossed and knees bent, so that if you were to sit up, you would move into a loose semblance of a meditation posture.

Bring your attention to your heart chakra and visualize the Tibetan syllable "hum" there. The syllable looks like this:

---

1. In Tibet, the traditional time to begin sleep yoga is 10 P.M. This means that the second stage of the practice coincides with midnight, while the third occurs some two hours before dawn. Although the timing here does not appear to be critical, it does suggest the Tibetan dream sages were well aware of their natural dream patterns.

You should imagine it as black, but luminous.[2] Begin a sequence of twenty-one deep breaths taken without strain, and allow your consciousness to merge with the "hum" syllable. Fall asleep in the merged state.

Although the fourth part of this practice is traditionally carried out two hours after the third and immediately before the first light of a Tibetan dawn, it is actually just as effective if you allow yourself to awaken naturally. If you are anything like I am first thing in the morning, you will be relieved to hear there are no special positions or breathing exercises. Instead you should simply get comfortable and focus your attention on your base chakra between your genitals and anus. Visualize a black luminous sphere at that point and again let your consciousness merge with it. Once you have done so, allow yourself to fall asleep again for a final period of cozy dreaming before you finally get up to face your working day.

Except, that is, your dreams (in this period at least) may be anything but cozy. All four stages of the practice are designed to manipulate your energies in ways that produce specific *types* of dreams.

The first, pre-sleep practice has the effect of generating peaceful, gentle dreams. The second practice, two hours later, carries the promise of transition consciousness and increased luminosity in the dream process, but even before that happens you should experience symbols of progress in the dream itself. Your dreams will suggest you are moving toward something and should be bright and enjoyable.

The third practice, involving the "hum" syllable, aims to develop your power; specifically, to put you in touch with the pre-existent power you have within yourself. With the contact comes a sense of security and the dreams generated reflect this.

---

2. The paradox involved in a luminous black object is less acute in the imaginal realm as you will see as soon as you attempt the visualization.

You may well find yourself in positions of authority or the object of approval from your peers.

The final practice tends to produce dreams that are far less pleasant, but just as important. The Tibetans refer to them as "wrathful" and you may find yourself overwhelmed by storms or floods or any one of a multitude of aggressive forces. In the West, dreams of this type are classified as nightmares and we do our best to forget them as quickly as possible. For the Tibetan dream yogi, they are opportunities to develop the quality of fearlessness.

Such a development naturally arises when you realize that however often your dream self is destroyed by the horrors of a wrathful dream, it somehow miraculously survives intact. The lesson is in many ways similar to the experience of the rite of Chöd in which you permit yourself to endure being utterly devoured. Familiarity with wrathful dreams will bring not contempt but a realization of the fact that, ultimately, nothing can actually harm you. This realization is, of course, intimately linked with the understanding that your sleeping environment, however solid it may seem, however terrifying it may appear, is nothing but a dream and hence the product of your own mind. In short, it is linked with lucidity.

Although lucidity is not the goal of Tibetan dream yoga, it is certainly a vital tool the Tibetan masters work hard to develop. Without lucidity, you are condemned to accept the illusion of reality all dreams present. With it, you can begin to make real spiritual progress. An ancient Tantric text gives this advice to those who achieve lucidity:

> At the outset, in the process of realizing it to be *maya* (illusion) abandon all feeling of fear; And, if the dream be of fire, transform the fire into water, the antidote of fire. And if the dream be of minute objects, transform them into large objects; Or if the dream be of large objects, transform them into small objects: Thereby

one comprehendeth the nature of dimensions. And if the dream be of a single thing, transform it into many things; Or if the dream be of many things, transform them into a single thing: Thereby one comprehendeth the nature of plurality and of unity.[3]

There are two reasons why the Tibetan practitioners seek this degree of dream control: one is associated with life, the other with death.

Toward the end of the seventeenth century, the self-styled "foolish monk" Lochen Dharma Shri had this to say about the development of dream lucidity:

> Apprehending the Dreams
> During the daytime, sustaining mindfulness without distraction
> Apart from the power of mental imprints, phenomena do not exist.
> All avenues of appearances, negative and affirmative,
> Are dream-like, though they are apprehended as external phenomena.
> Without distraction, earnestly and continually sustain your mindfulness
> And attention to this truth.[4]

This, as you can see, is a succinct expression of the techniques examined in chapter 12 designed to trigger lucidity by cultivating the mental habit of seeing your waking experience as a dream. Once the habit is ingrained, it will be carried into the dream state and lucidity results.

But Lochen's advice goes beyond this. The real thrust of dream yoga is to demonstrate *by experience* the truth of the Buddhist doctrine of maya, the same truth realized by those who doubt the reality of their yidam. When you become lucid in a dream, your dream environment appears no less real, no less

---

3. Quoted in W. Y. Evans-Wentz, *Tibetan Yoga and Secret Doctrines*.
4. Quoted in Gyatrul Rinpoche, *Ancient Wisdom*.

Chapter 13

solid, no less detailed. Indeed, if anything, the dream will often become more vivid than before. Yet by simply comprehending its actual nature, you can change it in any way you wish. You can, as the Tantric text states, change fire into water, turn large objects into small.

When you have done this a few times, it is almost inevitable that you will develop some deep reservations about the reality of your waking world. The idea that your daylight existence might also be an illusion is no longer an intellectual exercise designed to create the right mindset for lucid dreaming at night. Instead it gradually becomes a bred-in-the-bone conviction.

And here, although it is seldom spelled out to the uninitiated, is the single, central secret of Tibetan magic. If waking reality is a dream, then surely it can be manipulated just like the sleep dreams of the night? All that is really required is awareness of the truth.

With mastery of dream yoga comes the potential to change your waking circumstances at will. If the world is maya, or an illusion generated by your mind, then manipulation of your mind can change the nature of the illusion. As in your sleeping dreams, you can do anything you want—raise storms, change lead into gold, walk on water, all the astonishing talents attributed to magicians in every culture down the ages.

It is no coincidence that virtually every system of magic on the face of this planet is based on two basic premises: that you can do anything you *believe* you can do, and that clear, detailed visualization of a result will tend to bring that result about. Certainly for all the paraphernalia of ritual practice and talk of astral energies, these twin principles underlie the whole of the Western Esoteric Tradition. The training, trappings, and techniques serve only to support them. In the West, there is no clear theory about why magical methods should work, only the experience that, in certain hands, they do.

Yet magic, as anyone who has attempted its practice will confirm, is erratic; it is an art rather than a science. Without the basis of a valid theory, it is difficult to understand why. From Tibet, the answer comes swooping in. Basic belief in yourself and visualization of results will achieve results in direct proportion to your degree of realization that the world around you is unreal, the product of your mind.

Centuries ago, the people of Tibet embarked on an experiment that may have been unique in the history of our planet. They decided, as a culture, to give spiritual values a real chance. Where other nations paid lip-service, the Tibetans began to put principles into practice. They abandoned their warlike ways, ceased to covet the property of others, and turned inward. Eventually their veneration of the spiritual reached such a pitch that one person in every four of the entire population became a monk or nun; and almost all the rest saw themselves primarily as a support system.

Contrary to a great many Western fantasies, the experiment did not lead to an ideal society. As Professor Peter Bishop has pointed out, there was corruption in Tibet long before the Chinese invaded.[5] Even the Dalai Lama admits his beloved homeland was far too isolated and suffered from a cultural imbalance. But for all its faults, the leading edge of Tibetan spiritual practice produced some of the most remarkable insights into the nature of reality and the nature of mind that the world has ever known.

To some extent, the many magicians Tibet has produced are (more or less) like benign versions of the traitor in *The Matrix*. They realize the illusory nature of the world they inhabit, but prefer to change the dream rather than push through to the fearsome reality beyond. Many work to change the dream for

---

5. Bishop, *Dreams of Power.*

Chapter 13

the better by healing the sick and supporting the poor. A few attempt to change it for the worse by practicing what we would call black magic to increase their own comfort at the expense of their fellows.

Changing the dream for good or ill is a great temptation, but ultimately it is a fool's game. The world's most powerful sorcerer, whether saint or sinner, comes inevitably to face the futility of his or her existence at the moment of death. And this brings us directly to the second reason why Tibetan masters seek to practice dream control.

For those like Saint Milarepa who abandoned the magical path and sought instead to follow the mystical way, dream yoga has become an extraordinarily effective compass for negotiating the afterdeath state to achieve enlightenment and liberation from the wheel of birth, death, and rebirth. The "foolish monk" Lochen describes the process thus:

> The absorption of unification with the bardo state
> If, during the night, you familiarize yourself with the
>   inseparability
> Of the illusory body, the dream and the bardo state
> Imagine the play of the spiritual body through the gradual
>   dissolution
> Into the ultimate clear light of death.
> Imagine all self-arising deceptive appearances
> As the arisings of the illusory fulfilled body.
> Attend to the emptiness and lack of true existence of the entrance
>   ways
> And thus train in the ways of the emanation body.[6]

Although the language is a little obscure in parts, the overall thrust of the instruction is clear enough. Lochen Dharma Shri is advising his readers to practice for death, to stage a rehearsal in advance of the actual event. Dream yoga is the perfect way to do

6. Quoted, with minor changes, in Gyatrul Rinpoche, *Ancient Wisdom.*

The Practice of the Night

so since dreaming shares so many characteristics with the bardo state.

What Lochen is saying here is that by examining the mechanics of dreaming itself while in a lucid dream, you can come to understand how your dream body, your dream environment, and the underlying structure of your mind are all one and the same thing—body and environment are simply mental projections. This done, you can use the lucid dream to experience the gradual dissolution of your consciousness at death before you actually die. You can feel for yourself what it is like to slip into the clear light, then go on to interact with accurate mockups of the various bardo states that may arise. In this way, you train yourself to meet death in full consciousness of what is going on.

For practitioners of dream yoga, this training is an all-win situation, whatever their individual state of spiritual evolution. If your spiritual practice has brought you close to enlightenment, the training will allow you to pass without fear or revulsion directly into the clear light state when you die, and stay there. You will bypass the experience of the bardos. No longer will you need to reincarnate. Liberation and nirvana will be yours.

Less-evolved individuals still retain the possibility of enlightenment as well. Even if you are unable to hold yourself in the clear light state at first, your lucid dream rehearsals will at least enable you to recognize it, and to predict the immanent appearance of the illusory bardos. This realization in itself can be enough to permit you residence in the clear light, despite the small initial hiccough.

Since it is largely fear that drives people out of the clear light, even beginners can benefit from their experience of dream yoga. It allows them to understand that in the dreamlike death state there is nothing to fear and the "refuge" of reincarnation is an empty illusion. Sometimes that in itself can be enough to block the process of rebirth and allow the individual, with a little grit and determination, to seek out the realms of the clear light. For the Tibetan master, there is always hope.

EPILOGUE

How seriously should we take all this? The idea that magic works because life is an illusion runs contrary to the whole thrust of Western religious thought and almost all the Western-based philosophies. But it does receive support from one unexpected quarter: the world of physics.

It is sometimes remarked that public perceptions of science generally run about a century behind the actuality. If this is so, many people are likely to think of physics in terms of hard-nosed Victorian materialism that held that we live in a soulless universe of energy and matter. But this concept began to break down in the early years of the twentieth century when Einstein theorized that space and time were interlinked. Later, it cracked apart altogether with the advent of quantum mechanics.

Quantum mechanics is the best theory of physics humanity has ever developed. It explains more observed phenomena better than any other. Its fundamental tenets have been tested time and again. While it may not yet be able to explain absolutely everything, its insights into the nature of reality are profound. But the implications of those insights are quite extraordinary.

Atomic theory originally appeared in ancient Greece during the fifth century B.C.E. when philosophers like Democritus decided that if you cut something into smaller and smaller pieces you would eventually produce a piece so small you couldn't cut it any more. They called this tiny piece *atomos,* which means "indivisible."

For centuries atoms remained no more than a theory (although a theory with increasing evidence in its favor). Then, in the twentieth century, scientists not only confirmed the reality of atoms, but discovered that contrary to Greek thought, they could be split open, albeit with considerable difficulty. Inside were even smaller bits of matter that were promptly labelled subatomic particles.

Unfortunately, subatomic particles refused to behave like bits of matter. In one early experiment, a beam of them was directed toward a sensitized surface that registered their impact. A screen with two slits in it was placed between the source of the particles and the target. Each slit could be opened and closed independently. Common sense predicted that if both slits were opened, twice as many subatomic particles would get through than if you only opened one. By the end of the experiment, scientists had discovered more particles got through if only one slit is opened.

The experiment was repeated using light (which consists of subatomic particles called photons). Shining a light through a pinhole produces a circle of light on any screen beyond it. Two pinholes produce two circles of light. If they overlap there is an interference pattern that shows as alternating dark and light bands. But when the light source was reduced to emit only a single photon, the interference pattern remained with both pinholes open, although not with just one. So added to the question of how a single photon managed to interfere with itself, the scientists had to ask how it knew when two pinholes are open and not just one. (Einstein once remarked sourly that the photon must be telepathic.)

Another experiment involved something called a twin particle system with zero spin. A twin particle system is a thing complete in itself, not just a convenient marriage of two separate particles. Each particle in the system has its own spin, but the reason the system as a whole has no spin is that the spins of the two particles happen to be equal and opposite—in other words they cancel each other out.

Physicists discovered it was possible to separate the particles of such a system without influencing the spin factor. It was also possible to influence the spin of each individual particle by pushing it through a magnetic field. But if you did this, the spin of the twin particle also changed so the overall system remains at zero spin. The question was, how did the second particle "know" it had to change when the first was pushed through a magnetic field? The second particle didn't go through a magnetic field. Nothing was done to it at all. But it still changed. Clearly there was something amiss with thinking of particles as "little bits of matter."

There was a short-lived breakthrough when physicists had the idea that particles might not be little bits of matter at all, but rather energy waves. You can't observe subatomic particles directly, but only infer their nature by their behavior. Some of their behavior was certainly that of a wave-form, but not all. Sometimes particles behaved *exactly* like little bits of matter.

The problem didn't stop physicists from searching for the ultimate particle, the little bit of whatever-it-was that really would be the basic building block of matter that the ancient Greeks envisaged. For a while they theorized about quarks and leptons, but eventually they realized the entire solid, physical universe was made from nothing.

This is a chilling discovery. The ultimate bedrock of manifestation, which, of course, includes your physical body and mine, is a void filled with quantum foam made up of particles that emerge briefly from nothingness before disappearing again. Furthermore, whether anything exists at all is a question of probability rather than certainty.

A scientist named Werner Heisenberg developed this cornerstone of modern physics—usually called Heisenberg's Uncertainty Principle—on the observation that you cannot measure both the speed and the location of a subatomic particle. You can measure one or the other, but not both. The reason why you can't measure both is very strange—it's because you're looking at the particle. And once you observe one aspect—say the particle's location—you automatically and absolutely shut down any possibility of looking at the other. This means your mind, the human mind, or possibly just *mind* without qualification, is actively involved in the universe as a whole. It actually influences certain events at the quantum level. The outcome is that physicists have begun to postulate a basic unity of phenomena, the sort of *oneness* that mystics claim to be the ultimate reality.

Put all this together and what do you get? You get a phenomenal world that looks wonderfully solid but is ultimately an illusion created by the random motion of tiny bits of mystery that emerge from the void and return to the void in a perpetual dance influenced by the action of mind. That sounds suspiciously like Tibetan mysticism to me.

GLOSSARY

angkur—empowerment in a particular ability, usually as passed from teacher to pupil.

asura—denizen of the Demi-God Realm.

Baian-Kara-Ula—a Tibetan mountain range.

Bardo Thodol—*The Tibetan Book of the Dead.*

bardo—strictly a state of consciousness, but most often used to describe one of the between-lives states experienced by the individual after death.

Bön—aboriginal religion of Tibet.

Bönpoba—practitioner of Bön.

Buddha—"enlightened one." Usually refers to the last historical Buddha, Prince Gautama of India.

Chang Thang—a region of northern Tibet.

chang—ritual bell.

Chenresig—patron god of Tibet, believed to incarnate as the Dalai Lama.

Chöd—a rite of magical self-sacrifice.

Chöjung—Tibetan historical writings recorded in the thirteenth century.

dakini—a female spirit being.

Dalai Lama—secular and religious leader of Tibet.

damaru—small double drum.

dbu-ma—central energy channel of the human body.

189

Dorje Posture—Lotus Posture of hatha yoga.

dorje—ritual implement. Also sometimes used to denote the "diamond body" which represents the individual's Buddha nature or divine spark.

Dunkong Shakgyapa—early Buddhist scriptures.

Dzambu Lying—planet Earth.

Dzopa—Tibetan hill tribe who believe themselves to be the descendants of space-faring aliens.

Gomchen—mystic title translating as "great hermit."

ham—letter of the Tibetan alphabet.

hdab-ston—crown chakra.

hum—Tibetan symbol for divine life force.

Jigten Chagtsul—Tibetan scriptures.

Kanchenjunga—world's second highest mountain; also known as K2.

kangling—human thighbone trumpet.

Kargyut-pa—school of Tibetan Buddhism founded by the Tibetan saint Marpa.

khor ba—suffering; equivalent to Indian term *sangsara*.

khor-lo—energy center (chakra) of the human body.

kylkhor—magic circle.

la—Tibetan syllable.

lama—Tibetan monk.

Lha—alien race that evolved into humanity.

Lhasa—the Tibetan capital.

lung-gom-pa—Tibetan trance runner.

maheketang—ceremonial runner who chases demons.

mala—Tibetan rosary.

mandala—balanced design motif used in meditation.

nirvana—state achieved when an individual resolves all dualities and ceases to incarnate.

om—mantric sound supposed to reflect the keynote of the universe.

Panchen Lama—second most senior lama of Tibet, next to the Dalai Lama.

Glossary

phurba—ceremonial dart.

pustaka—small ceremonial image of a sacred book.

ra—Tibetan syllable.

repa—light cotton robe. Also, by derivation, the title given to a tumo adept.

rigpa—the experience of nonduality.

Rinpoche—mystic title translating as "precious one."

Rirab Lhunpo—home planet of the Lha.

rkyang-ma—left-hand energy channel of the human body.

rlung—the energy that runs through the rtsa channels; equivalent to the ch'i of Chinese acupuncture.

ro-ma—right-hand energy channel of the human body.

rtsa—energy channel of the human body.

sa—Tibetan syllable.

samadhi—ecstatic trance state often believed to be a prelude to nirvana.

sang-na—root chakra.

sankha—ceremonial conch shell used as a musical instrument.

sha—Tibetan syllable.

Shalu Gompa—Tibetan monastery that specializes in lung-gom-pa training.

shugs—the energy contained in semen.

thangka—painting of protection of the Buddha.

thig-li—subtle essences pervading each human being.

tingshaw—ceremonial cymbal.

trisula—ceremonial trident.

tulpa—thought form entity.

tumo—a form of yoga characterized by the generation of body heat.

Vajra-Yogini—Tantric goddess.

yidam—tutelary deity.

zhiné—contemplative meditation.

WORKS CITED

Ashcroft-Nowicki, Dolores, and J. H. Brennan. *Magical Use of Thought Forms*. St. Paul, Minn.: Llewellyn Publications, 2001.

Bishop, Peter. *Dreams of Power*. London: Athlone Press, 1993.

Brennan, J. H. *Discover Reincarnation*. London: Aquarian Press, 1992.

———. *A Secret History of Ancient Egypt*. London: Piatkus, 2000.

Butler, W. E. *The Magician: His Training and Work*. London: Aquarian Press, 1963.

Clifford, Terry. *Tibetan Buddhist Medicine and Psychiatry*. York Beach, Maine: Samuel Weiser, Inc., 1990.

Collins, Andrew. *Gods of Eden*. London: Headline, 1998.

David-Neel, Alexandra. *Bandits, Priests, and Demons*. The Hague: Uitgeverij Sirius en Siderius, 1988.

———. *Initiations and Initiates in Tibet*. London: Rider, 1970.

———. *Magic and Mystery in Tibet*. London: Souvenir Press, 1967.

David-Neel, Alexandra, and Lama Yongden. *The Secret Oral Teachings in Tibetan Buddhist Sects*. San Francisco: City Lights, 1971.

Evans-Wentz, W. Y. *Tibet's Great Yogi Milarepa: A Biography from the Tibetan*. London: Oxford University Press, 1951.

Evans-Wentz, W. Y., ed. *Tibetan Yoga and Secret Doctrines*. London: Oxford University Press, 1969.

193

Ford, Robert. *Captured in Tibet*. London: Pan Books, 1958.

Govinda, Lama Anagarika. *Foundations of Tibetan Mysticism*. York Beach, Maine: Samuel Weiser, Inc., 1969.

Guiley, Rosemary Ellen. *Harper's Encyclopedia of Mystical and Paranormal Experience*. San Francisco: HarperSanFrancisco, 1991.

Gyatrul Rinpoche. *Ancient Wisdom*. Ithaca, N.Y.: Snow Lion Publications, 1993.

Illion, Theodor. *In Secret Tibet*. Stelle, Ill.: Adventures Unlimited Press, 1991.

Houston, Jean. *The Hero and the Goddess*. London: Aquarian Press, 1993.

Jansen, Eva Rudy. *Singing Bowls*. Diever, Holland: Binkey Kok Publications, 1997.

Kelder, Peter. *Tibetan Secrets of Youth and Vitality*. Wellingborough, England: Aquarian Press, 1988.

Kjellson, Henry. *Försvunnen teknik*. Copenhagen: Nihil, 1961.

LaBerge, Stephen. *Lucid Dreaming*. New York: Ballantine, 1985.

Landon, Perceval. *Lhasa*. 2 vols. London: Hurst and Blackett, 1905.

Norbu, Namkhai. *Dream Yoga and the Practice of Natural Light*. Ithaca, N.Y.: Snow Lion Publications, 1992.

Norbu, Thubten Jigme, and Colin Turnbull. *Tibet: Its History, Religion, and People*. London: Pelican Books, 1972.

Paijmans, Theo. *Free Energy Pioneer: John Worrel Keely*. Lilburn, Ga.: IllumiNet Press, 1998.

Robin-Evans, Karyl. *Sungods in Exile*. London: Sphere Books, 1980.

Stowell, Mary S. "Precognitive Dreams: A Phenomenological Study." *Journal of the American Society for Psychical Research* 91 (1997):163. Quoted in William Corless, *Science Frontiers* (Ann Arbor, Mich.: The Sourcebook Project, 2000).

Thurman, Robert A. F., trans. *The Tibetan Book of the Dead*. London: Aquarian Press, 1994.

van Eeden, Frederik. "A Study of Dreams." *Proceedings of the Society for Psychical Research* 26 (1913).

Wangyal Rinpoche, Tenzin. *The Tibetan Yogas of Dream and Sleep.* Ithaca, N.Y.: Snow Lion Publications, 1998.

Watson, Lyall. *Supernature.* London: Hodder & Staughton, 1973.

INDEX

energy centers, 38
energy waves, 187
England, xvi, 86
enlightenment, 15, 42, 53, 102,
    104, 110–111, 160, 181–182
entrainment, 51–52
esoteric tumo, 59
ether, 28, 40, 43, 65
Europe, xvii, 20, 57, 85, 139
Evans-Wentz, W. Y., 14, 67,
    70–71, 74, 178
evening review, 166
Everest, Mount, 9, 16
Eye of Revelation, The, 114
eyes, 41, 46, 54, 57, 59, 64, 95,
    100, 117, 142, 154, 162,
    170

F

falling spirits, 136
First World War, 20, 86
Forceful Zhiné, 161, 163
Ford, Robert, 19
fountain of youth, 113–114
Four Combined Breathing, 70
Försvunnen teknik, 22
France, 20, 26, 86
French Geographical Society, 25
Freud, Sigmund, 84
frontal cortex, 10–11

G

Galations, 105
gall bladder, 40
gall ducts, 40

Gavraud, Professor, 26–27
Gennadius, Saint, 138
God, 7, 105, 120, 158
God Realm, 109–110, 158
goddess, 39, 61–63, 72, 78, 82,
    115, 117
Goddess of All-Fulfilling Wis-
    dom, 115
gold, 25, 31, 34, 179
Gomchen, 20–21
Great Liberation, see *Book of
    the Great Liberation*
Great Pyramid, 74
Greece, 71, 185
gross consciousness, 46
guardian, xvi
Guirdham, Arthur, 86
Gupta, Reena, 83
guru, 55–56, 60–62, 67–68,
    111–112, 117–126, 159, 164

H

Haggard, H. Rider, 113
Hamadan, *see* Ecbatana
Harte, R., 31
hatha yoga, 64, 115
hdab-ston, 42
heart, 39–41, 43, 45–46, 49,
    53, 65, 67, 73, 75, 78,
    99–101, 130, 158, 170, 173,
    175
Heisenberg, Werner, 187
Hell Realm, 109–110, 158
Hemis Monastery, 25
higher consciousness, 42
Hilton, James, 6, 113

M

204

Practice of the Night, 161, 169, 171, 173, 175, 177, 179, 181, 183
prayer flag, xiv
Prayer Formula of the Six Doctrines, 68
psychic channels, 44–45, 73
psychic powers, 42
psychometry, 22, 25
pustaka, xiv

Q

quantum mechanics, 185
quarks, 187
quartz crystal, 148

R

"ra," 174
readiness wave, 11
reality check, 153
reality testing, 152, 164
recurring dreams, 150
Red Hat sect, 18
Reeves, Keanu, 127–128
regression, 84–87, 90–94, 98, 100, 111
reincarnation, 7–8, 15, 18–19, 81–85, 87, 89–93, 95–98, 102, 105, 109–112, 115–116, 182
REM sleep, 130–131, 145
repa, 16, 59, 77
respiratory system, 40
rigor mortis, 100
rigpa, 160

Rirab Lhunpo, 2
rkyang-ma, 37–38, 66, 73
rlung, 44–46, 56, 157–161
ro-ma, 37–38, 66, 73
Robin-Evans, Karyl, 3
Roman Circus, 84
root guru, 67–68
Royal Belgian Geographical Society, 25
rtsa, 37–38, 42, 44–45, 59, 72–73, 101, 170

S

"sa," 174
sacral plexus, 39–40
sacred music, 51
sahasrara, 40–42
samadhi, 16
Sambhava, Padma, 98–99
sang-na, 42
sangsara, 115–116, 129
sankha, xiv
Sanskrit, 38, 63, 121
Saturn, 35
Second World War, xvi, 109, 139
Secret Place, *see sang-na*
seminal ducts, 40
sending a wish, 166
Senoi, 133–136, 138–139, 147
sense organs, 41
"sha," 174
Shalu Gompa Monastery, 55
shamanic drumming, 52
Shangri-La, 6
Shantarakshita, 98

205

Tibetan Book of the Dead, 98,
    103–104, 111
Tibetan Buddhism, xiii, 15, 18,
    99
Tibetan Esoteric Tradition, xiii,
    81, 115
Tibetan magic, xvii, 179
Tibetan medicine, 37
Tibetan mysticism, xvii, 188
Tibetan plateau, xvi, 3, 58
tin, 34–35
tingshaw, xiv
Tohats, 135
tongue, xix, 41, 64, 69, 100
trance, xix, 19, 42, 52, 54–58,
    82, 87–88, 90, 93–94, 122,
    135, 163
Transcendental Meditation, 55
Triangle of Evocation, 119–120
Trisong Detsen, 98
trisula, xiv
Tsum Um Nui, 3
tulpa, 21, 123
tumo, 16, 20–21, 59–61, 63,
    65, 67–69, 71–73, 75–79,
    115, 117, 129; see also eso-
    teric tumo, mystic tumo
Turkey, 89
twin particle system, 186

U

Ultimate Zhiné, 161, 164
Uncertainty Principle, 187
unconditional love, 42
United States, 83, 114; see also
    America

University of Virginia, 89
unreality check, 165–166
unseen companion, 9–10
upper intestine, 40
urinary ducts, 40

V

Vajra-Dhara, 68
Vajra-Yogini, 62–63, 72, 76, 78
van Eeden, Frederik, 141–143
Venus, 35, 50, 92
Verwey, Joey, 83
vibrational lift, 31
Victorian materialism, 185
Violent Breathing, 71
visualization, 21, 39, 57,
    63–66, 71–73, 75, 77–79,
    115, 122–124, 151–152,
    161, 173, 175–176,
    179–180
visuddha, 40, 42
Voodoo, 52

W

W.I.L.D., 153
Walter, W. Grey, 10–11
Watson, Lyall, 26
Western Esoteric Tradition, 72,
    77, 82, 119, 179
Wheel of Bliss, 43, 53
Wheel of Enjoyment, 43
Wheel of Phenomena, 43
Wheel of the Preservation of
    Happiness, 43, 60
Wheel of Transmutation, 43

wheel, xiii–xiv, xxi, 7, 38–39, 43, 53, 57, 60, 62, 102, 110, 113, 115, 117, 119, 121, 123, 125–126, 167, 181
White Cave of the Horse's Tooth, 16
white light, 71, 175
witchcraft, 119
World War I, *see* First World War
World War II, *see* Second World War
wrathful deities, 65, 111
wrathful goddess, 117

X

Xanthus, 87–89

Y

Yellow Hat sect, 18
Yetse Tsogyal, 98
yidam, 118–119, 121–126, 178
yoga, 10, 20, 42, 55–56, 59, 64, 67–68, 70, 76, 78, 81, 115, 160, 170, 175, 178
Yongden, 54
Younghusband Expedition, 17
Yungtun-Trogyal, 14

Z

Zen, 7
zhiné, 161, 163–164, 173; *see also* Forceful Zhiné, Natural Zhiné, Ultimate Zhiné

☾ REACH FOR THE MOON

Llewellyn publishes hundreds of books on your favorite subjects! To get these exciting books, including the ones on the following pages, check your local bookstore or order them directly from Llewellyn.

Order by Phone
- Call toll-free within the U.S. and Canada, 1-877-NEW-WRLD
- In Minnesota, call (651) 291-1970
- We accept VISA, MasterCard, and American Express

Order by Mail
- Send the full price of your order (MN residents add 7% sales tax) in U.S. funds, plus postage & handling to:
  Llewellyn Worldwide
  P.O. Box 64383, Dept. 0-7387-0067-3
  St. Paul, MN 55164–0383, U.S.A.

Postage & Handling
- **Standard** (U.S., Mexico, & Canada)

If your order is:

$20.00 or under, add $5.00

$20.01–$100.00, add $6.00

Over $100, shipping is free

(Continental U.S. orders ship UPS. AK, HI, PR, & P.O. Boxes ship USPS 1st class. Mex. & Can. ship PMB.)

- **Second Day Air** (Continental U.S. only): $10.00 for one book + $1.00 per each additional book
- **Express** (AK, HI, & PR only) [Not available for P.O. Box delivery. For street address delivery only.]: $15.00 for one book + $1.00 per each additional book
- **International Surface Mail:** Add $1.00 per item
- **International Airmail:** Books—Add the retail price of each item; Non-book items—Add $5.00 per item

Please allow 4–6 weeks for delivery on all orders.
Postage and handling rates subject to change.

Discounts
We offer a 20% discount to group leaders or agents. You must order a minimum of 5 copies of the same book to get our special quantity price.

FREE CATALOG

Get a free copy of our color catalog, *New Worlds of Mind and Spirit*. Subscribe for just $10.00 in the United States and Canada ($30.00 overseas, airmail). Call 1-877-NEW-WRLD today!

Visit our website at www.llewellyn.com for more information.

Magical Use of Thought Forms

DOLORES ASHCROFT-NOWICKI
& J. H. BRENNAN

Two leading occult researchers present the most comprehensive training manual on how to create thought forms through astral manipulation. It includes sections on the structure of reality as well as new visualization techniques that will train your inner eye to build correct images.

You will learn the three-point location of occult power in the physical brain, how to build up desire as fuel for a potent astral engine, and how to control what you create. Advanced astral structures are also covered, including God-forms and Angelics, audial images, and astral landscapes.

Perhaps the most spectacular aspect of the book is the instruction given for the performance of the legendary alchemical experiment: the creation of the homunculus, an animated form that can last up to several hours.

- Two well-known authors team up to create the definitive reference work on thought forms
- The heart of the book lies in the powerful techniques, some never before in print, for creating mental forms to attract power for practical use
- For magical practitioners of any tradition

1-56718-084-1
256 pp., 7½ x 9⅛ $14.95

Magick for Beginners
The Power to Change Your World

J. H. BRENNAN

Many magicians wear a great cloak, "the aura of dark mystery," which J. H. Brennan endeavors to remove in *Magick for Beginners*. In doing so, he introduces many aspects of magic and the occult, and explains in detail several experiments which you can try for yourself, including producing a $100 bill by magic and becoming invisible.

The book is divided into two parts: Low Magick and High Magick. In Low Magick you will explore the Ouija board, astral and etheric bodies, the chakras, the aura, Qabalah, wood nymphs and leprechauns, mantra chanting, water and ghost divining, and the Tree of Life. Low Magick is fun, and serves as an introduction to the more potent system of High Magick. Here you will learn how to correctly prepare your mind before conducting ritual magic and how to conduct the rituals themselves.

1–56718–086–8
336 pp., 5³⁄₁₆ x 8, illus.

$9.95

The Magical I Ching

J. H. BRENNAN

It's the oldest book in the world . . . yet scholars disagree about its age. It has been consulted by millions in the Orient . . . yet no more than a handful have ever read it all. It is revered for its wisdom . . . yet it is used to tell fortunes.

Using coins, yarrow stalks, or even a computer, you can cast fortunes using six-lined figures known as hexagrams. This wholly new translation of the ancient Chinese *I Ching* helps you interpret the hexagrams, whose meanings continue to be useful throughout the ages, providing profound and strikingly accurate divinations.

More than a divination tool, the *I Ching* also has links with the Astral Plane and the Spirit World. Use it in ritual and pathworking, as an astral doorway or a spirit guide. Although there are many versions of the *I Ching* on the market, this is the first to delve into the magical techniques that underlie the oracle.

1-56718-087-6
264 pp., 7½ x 9⅛   **$14.95**

Spanish edition:
La magia del I Ching
1-56718-083-3   **$14.95**

Time Travel
A New Perspective

J. H. BRENNAN

Scattered throughout the world are the skeletal remains of men and women from long before humanity appeared on the planet, and a human footprint contemporary with the dinosaurs. Where did they come from? Are these anomalies the litter left by time travelers from our own distant future? *Time Travel* is an extraordinary trip through some of the most fascinating discoveries of archaeology and physics, indicating that not only is time travel theoretically possible, but that future generations may actually be engaged in it. In fact, the latest findings of physicists show that time travel, at a subatomic level, is already taking place. Unique to this book is the program—based on esoteric techniques and the findings of parapsychology and quantum physics—which enables you to structure your own group investigation into a form of vivid mental time travel.

1-56718-085-X
224 pp., 6 x 9, photos $12.95

The Eastern Mysteries

An Encyclopedic Guide to the Sacred Languages & Magickal Systems of the World

DAVID ALLEN HULSE

Formerly titled *The Key of It All–Book One.*

The Eastern Mysteries (companion guide to *The Western Mysteries*) clarifies and extends the knowledge established by all previous books on occult magick. This book catalogs and distills, in hundreds of tables of secret symbolism, the true alphabet magick of every ancient Eastern magickal tradition: Cuneiform, Hebrew, Arabic, Sanskrit, Tibetan, and Chinese. Unlike the current rash of publications which do no more than recapitulate Regardie or Crowley, *The Eastern Mysteries* series establishes a new level of competence in all fields of magick both East and West. It is a one-stop shop for the underlying information on magick, and the essential sourcebook for the composition of rituals.

1-56718-428-6
656 pp., 7 x 10 $29.95

To order, call 1-877-NEW-WRLD
Prices subject to change without notice

9 Days to Change Your Life

KARMA MANUAL

DR. JONN MUMFORD
(Swami Anandakapila Saraswati)

The Karma Manual
9 Days to Change Your Life

DR. JONN MUMFORD
(SWAMI ANANDAKAPILA SARASWATI)

Many Westerners talk about karma, but few really know much about it. Now Dr. Jonn Mumford provides a clear, practical guide, featuring the traditional yet innovative approach of his first guru, Dr. Swami Gitananda Giti of India.

Karma is a simple law of consequence, not of moralistic retribution and penalty. It's a way of viewing existence that results in increased mental health and self-responsibility.

Discover the different types of karma. Process your personal karma by clearing out unwanted automatic actions—thus lessening the amount and rate at which new karma accumulates. Finally, learn a very direct method for "deep frying" the karmic seeds in your being through the Nine-Day Karma Clearing Program.

1-56718-490-1
216 pp., 5³⁄₁₆ x 8   **$9.95**

Death: Beginning or End?

Methods for Immortality

DR. JONN MUMFORD
(SWAMI ANANDAKAPILA SARASWATI)

This book is an exhilarating celebration of life—and death. It is a thought-provoking and interactive tool that will alter your perceptions about death and prepare you for reincarnation. Explore the history of death rituals and attitudes from other ages and cultures. Uncover surprising facts about this inevitable life event. Moreover, discover the *ultimate truth* about death, knowledge that is guaranteed to have a profound impact on how you live the rest of your life!

Learn how your experience of life *after birth* will impact your experience of life after death. Personally engage in five "alchemical laboratories"—five of the most crucial "stocktaking" exercises you will ever do. Learn a traditional Hindu meditation that will provide a psychic and mental refuge as well as deep physical relaxation. Practice a mantra that can liberate you from the endless wheel of blind incarnation. Use the tools provided in the book and avoid the death's biggest tragedy: to not ever discover who you are in life.

1-56718-476-6
224 pp., 5³⁄₁₆ x 6 $9.95

Psychic Development for Beginners
An Easy Guide to Releasing and Developing Your Psychic Abilities

WILLIAM W. HEWITT

Psychic Development for Beginners provides detailed instruction on developing your sixth sense, or psychic ability. Improve your sense of worth, your sense of responsibility, and therefore your ability to make a difference in the world. Innovative exercises like "The Skyscraper" allow beginning students of psychic development to quickly realize personal and material gain through their own natural talent.

Benefits range from the practical to spiritual. Find a parking space anywhere, handle a difficult salesperson, choose a compatible partner, and even access different time periods! Practice psychic healing on pets or humans—and be pleasantly surprised by your results. Use psychic commands to prevent dozing while driving. Preview out-of-body travel, cosmic consciousness, and other alternative realities. Instruction in *Psychic Development for Beginners* is supported by personal anecdotes, forty-four psychic development exercises, and twenty-eight related psychic case studies to help students gain a comprehensive understanding of the psychic realm.

1-56718-360-3
216 pp., 5¼ x 8 $9.95

Energy Focused Meditation
Body, Mind, Spirit

GENEVIEVE LEWIS PAULSON

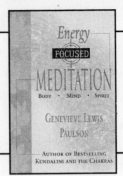

Formerly titled *Meditation and Human Growth*.

Meditation has many purposes: healing, past life awareness, balance, mental clarity, and relaxation. It is a way of opening into areas that are beyond your normal thinking patterns. In fact, what we now call "altered states" and "peak experiences"—tremendous experiences of transcendental states—can become normal occurrences when you know how to contact the higher energy vibrations.

Most people think that peak experiences happen, at best, only a few times in life. Through meditation, however, it is possible to develop your higher awareness so you can bring more peak happenings about by concentrated effort. *Energy Focused Meditation* is full of techniques for those who wish to claim those higher vibrations and expanded awareness for their lives today.

1-56718-512-6
224 pp., 6 x 9, 17 illus. $12.95